EATING
LAS VEGAS

EATING LAS VEGAS

THE 50 ESSENTIAL RESTAURANTS

John Curtas | Max Jacobson | Al Mancini

Huntington Press
Las Vegas, Nevada

EATING LAS VEGAS
The 50 Essential Restaurants

Published by
Huntington Press
3665 Procyon St.
Las Vegas, NV 89103
Phone (702) 252-0655
e-mail: books@huntingtonpress.com

Copyright ©2010, John Curtas, Max Jacobson, Al Mancini

ISBN: 978-1-935396-39-0
Library of Congress Control Number: 2010935131
$12.95us

Cover Photo: BARMASA—MGM Resorts International
Author Photo: Denise Truscello
Inside Photos: Spoon ©Torsten Schon, Dreamstime; MGM Resorts International: pgs. vi, 10, 16, 18, 20, 24, 26, 28, 30, 32, 38, 42, 50, 52, 64, 68, 74, 82, 86, 100, 108, 133, 136, 137; Wynn Las Vegas and Encore, pgs. 8, 12, 92, 129; Venetian/Palazzo, pgs. 14, 34, 40, 44, 104; Caesars Palace: pgs. 22, 36; 70, 78; Bill Hughes: pgs. 46, 54, 56, 58, 62, 76, 84, 96, 135; Paris, Las Vegas: pgs. 48, 139; Marché Bacchus: pg. 60; N9NE Group: pgs. 66, 128; Boyd Gaming: pg. 72, Rosemary's: pg. 80; Settebello: pg. 88; Palms/Palms Place: pgs. 90, 127; Wolfgang Puck Fine Dining Group: pgs. 94, 112; Todd's Unique Dining: pg. 98; Stratosphere: pg. 102; Vintner Grill: pg. 106; Firefly Tapas: pg. 124; Circus Circus: pg. 125; Golden Steer: pg. 126; Denise Truscello: pg. 129; Harrah's Las Vegas: pg. 130; Lettuce Entertain You Restaurants: pg. 131; Ciao Ciao: pg. 132; John Curtas: pgs. 134, 135; Richard Brian Photography: pg. 137; Yard House: pg. 138; M Resort: pg. 139; Downtown Cocktail Room pg. 140
Production & Design: Laurie Cabot

Acknowledgments

The authors would like to thank Amy Rossetti and Alex Acuna of Cosmpolitan Las Vegas, Debbie Munch and Celena Haas at Harrah's, Alyssa Bushey at the Mandarin Oriental, Andrea Brown and Suzie Rugh at MGM Resorts, Larry Fink at the Palms, Dawn Britt and Amy Carlson at the Venetian and Palazzo, and Katie Conway at Wynn Las Vegas and Encore, as well as all of their staffs, for their help not only with this book, but with countless projects over the years.

Similarly, we would like to thank the entire staffs of Kirvin Doak Communications, Langdon Flynn Communication, Magnetic Public Relations, Margolis Marketing Concepts, P.R. Plus, Preferred Public Relations, and R&R Partners for their tireless work on behalf of so many of Las Vegas' finest restaurants, and the Las Vegas Convention and Visitors Authority for all of its work to help elevate Las Vegas to its status as one of the world's finest dining destinations.

And finally, we want to thank all of the employees in the kitchens, front-of-the-houses, and corporate offices of each and every restaurant listed in this book for providing us with so many incredible meals.

Dedications

To my parents who made me, my sons who improved me,
and the Food Gal who puts up with me,
I hereby dedicate my humble portion of this book.
—John Curtas

To my patient wife, Setu, and to all the schnorrer
wannabes out there who think they could do my job.
—Max Jacobson

To my parents, for not subscribing to my belief that
children don't belong in restaurants, and for buying me
that graduation dinner at Daniel that began my long and
expensive journey into the world of fine dining.
And to my wife Sue, who will always be my
favorite dinner date and the only editor I really trust.
—Al Mancini

Tuna-Raspberry Skewer at Julian Serrano, ARIA

Contents

Introduction

Writing this book was a lot of fun—if you consider three guys with massive egos shouting one another down, mocking opinions, and generally trying to one-up each other at any opportunity to be fun. Fortunately, we do. Because for all of our differences, whether in age, area of expertise, level of experience, or food preferences, we all share an immense amount of respect for each other's abilities and a love of talking about all things food-related.

Our differences, however, inspired this book. As the restaurant critics for Las Vegas' three alternative weekly newspapers, we write for three surprisingly different audiences. And we do it using drastically different voices, which will be obvious to anyone who flips through even a few entries in this book. But most importantly, while we all have a well-rounded knowledge of every type of food, our propensities are drastically different.

Max, who's as well-traveled as he is well-written, could probably spend half his life in authentic hole-in-the-wall ethnic dives, augmented by the occasional visit to a world-class fine-dining establishment. His time spent in Southeast Asia, Europe, and South America, and as restaurant critic for the *L.A. Times,* has left him with an encyclopedic knowledge of food from around the world, which he's more than willing to share with anyone within earshot.

John, our resident food snob, who writes in the royal "we," is practically addicted to haute cuisine. And he can analyze a massive wine list as well as many of Las Vegas' best sommeliers—before inevitably bitching about the prices. But he wouldn't be caught dead in a lot of the delicious greasy spoons his coauthors are known to frequent.

And Al has spent so much time backstage at rock concerts that he's deluded himself into thinking he's actually a rock star himself, boasting the only multi-colored Mohawk and tattooed head you're likely to see in a Michelin-starred restaurant. He's usually the first to know where the cool kids are hanging out, although he sometimes seems more concerned with finding the hip crowd than with what they're eating.

Any one of us could easily put together a list of 50 essential restaurants. In fact, we each did just that when we started this project. (OK, John wrote up a list of 100; brevity has never been his strong suit!) But because of our differences in styles and backgrounds, we each have our fans and detractors. So, if any one of us had tried to write this book individually, it would have been embraced by the people who enjoy our individual writing and quickly dismissed by those who hate us. But if we could come up with 50 essential restaurants on which we could all *agree*, we figured a few more people might take it seriously. And with the exception of a handful of adamant vetoes, no chef who didn't make the list will ever know who was pulling for him and who was leaning against in the selection process.

We've been asked many times to explain what we mean by the word "essential." It's probably best defined by saying these are the restaurants that show off the broad spectrum of dining available in Las Vegas, arguably one of the finest restaurant cities in the United States. In other words, if you eat your way through this entire book, you'll get to see the breadth and depth of quality dining available in our town.

It's important to note we avoided declaring these the "best" restaurants in Las Vegas. Any traditional ranking of food, service, and décor would have left us with a list populated almost entirely by fine French restaurants and super-pricey steakhouses. Las Vegas certainly has enough of those to fill an entire book. But we believe the typical reader doesn't want to eat exclusively at that type of establishment. When our friends and relatives come to town, they ask us to recommend a variety of restaurants: a casual coffee shop, great dim sum, a good poolside meal, a classic old-Vegas experience, or a place for a quiet romantic dinner, all within various budgets. So this book represents that variety, offering what we feel are the best eateries in each of those many categories.

Thus, the book is divided into three sections. The first lists our top-ten restaurants based on traditional standards and listed alphabetically. They are, quite simply, the best places in town. Any one of them will deliver a once-in-a-lifetime meal every time you dine there. And most of them will drain your wallet and fill your stomach to such a degree that both bank account and waistline will prohibit visitors from eating at more than one or two of them per visit. But each is guaranteed to be one of the highlights of any trip to Las Vegas and to make any special occasion unforgettable.

The other 40 of our "essential" restaurants, also arranged alphabetically, include all of the other types of restaurants we love. There is something here for every taste and we all feel comfortable recommending each of them. These are the places we yelled about over many a meal, while curious waiters and waitresses tried to eavesdrop on our conversations and Tweet what they heard to their friends in the restaurant business. But those arguments were more about the overall balance of the book—did we want more ethnic restaurants, an extra steakhouse, or one more hipster hangout?—than the quality of any given place.

There were a few not-so-friendly debates, however—times when one or two of us felt a place just *had* to be included and someone else vehemently put his foot down and refused. And since unanimous consent was required for inclusion on the list, one man's veto was enough to keep an establishment off of it. But for the most argued-about places that didn't make the final cut, we've included a short veto section. Here, you'll find the comments of the restaurant's most ardent supporter and most vehement critic. We hope that the proprietors and chefs of the vetoed establishments realize that they were a step away from inclusion in the 50, which puts them right there with the elite.

All of our 50 essential restaurants, as well as those in the veto section, are categorized by price. It's important to note that these are rough estimates, since it's always possible to go hog wild and run up a massive bill or to seek out bargains and get out of a place for less than the average check. The book's pricing structure is based on an appetizer, an entrée, a side or dessert, and one or two cocktails or glasses of the more reasonably priced wine. For the most part, restaurants described as "inexpensive" will set you back less than $25 per person for dinner. Those rated "moderate" will cost between $25 and $75 a head. You should expect to spend between $75 and $125 apiece at the restaurants labeled "expensive." And the "very expensive" places will easily cost more than $125 per person—and often several times that amount. For easy reference, we've compiled the pricing parameters in a table that appears at the end of this introduction. Remember, these days restaurants have websites, most of which list complete menus and prices, if you want specifics; the websites are listed at the top of each review.

Finally, we've included a chapter of lists in the back of the book. They offer our suggestions for a great pizza, burger, and beer selection, along with several other categories about which we're frequently asked. Many might not live up to the criteria to make the essential 50. But it's a handy guide if you're looking for something specific.

It's also worth noting that, given the nature of the restaurant business, some of our early choices for inclusion in this book had to be cut at the last minute. A few simply closed their doors, while others lost the chefs who had made them famous. But the more difficult decisions came when we learned through the grapevine that some of our favorite restaurants would be re-tooling their concepts—most notable among them Fleur de Lys at Mandalay Bay, Bradley Ogden at Caesars Palace, and the Fat Greek, a family-owned-and-operated west-side Greek restaurant.

We'd also be remiss not to mention that shortly after this book hits stores, the new Cosmopolitan will open, boasting numerous great restaurants that will undoubtedly be in the running for our next edition. It remains to be seen whether the lineup of Scott Conant's Scarpetta, Estatorios Milos, Jose Andres' Jaleo, Blue Ribbon, David Myer's Comme Ça, and (of course) the obligatory steakhouse and burger bar will be a game-changer.

For now, we believe *Eating Las Vegas* provides the best guide to 50 restaurants you can enjoy today. Despite all the debates, the three of us are extremely proud of this list. And if you can get the three of *us* to agree, we have no doubt you will too.

Bon appétit!

Price Designations

Based on appetizer, entrée, a side or dessert, and one or two lower-priced cocktails per person.

Inexpensive	$25 or less
Moderate	$25 to $75
Expensive	$75 to $125
Very Expensive	$125 and up

Foreword

The dining-out scene in Las Vegas is always in flux. The competition is so stiff and the stakes are high for restaurants that have star chefs' names on the door and millions of dollars invested in the décor. For more than 10 years, a Vegas restaurant has had to be much more than just a good place to eat, as had been the case for decades before; now, a restaurant has to compete with international marquee names like Alain Ducasse, Guy Savoy, and Joël Robuchon, not to mention stellar American names like Brad Ogden, Rick Moonen, and Wolfgang Puck—all with restaurants in town.

Making sense of who's on top, who's surging, and who's rumored to be closing in Vegas takes both a gargantuan appetite and an indefatigable energy for dining out, lunch and dinner. It also takes a keen curiosity to find the real story behind the public statements, someone with a good Rolodex, and a lawyer's acumen for extracting the truth. Fortunately, the authors of *Eating Las Vegas* have all that—if you'll pardon a pun—in spades.

Such formidable tasks have taken the time and abilities of John Curtas, Max Jacobson, and Al Mancini to come up with the 50 "essential" restaurants in the city that every gourmet, gourmand, feinschmecker, nosher, and food dude needs to know. Each writer brings his own perspective, which doesn't always jibe with his colleagues', as to which restaurants have made Vegas into the grand dining city it has become.

Unlike so many restaurant guides whose commentators are faceless and deliberately devoid of personality, the three experts here are never shy about giving real punch to their assessments. Since there is *no* such thing as objectivity when it comes to restaurant reviewing, the fierce subjectivity of Curtas, Jacobson, and Mancini makes *Eating Las Vegas* authoritative, colorful, and so damn fun to read.

Had I the time and lots of money, I'd start on page one and eat my way through all 50 restaurants here, pretty sure that, even if I don't always get a great meal, I'll have plenty to argue about with my three friends.

—John Mariani, Food and Travel Columnist for *Esquire*

Section I
The Top Ten

ALEX (Strip)

Wynn Las Vegas
(702) 248-3463
wynnlasvegas.com
Wed.-Sat., 6-10 p.m.
Very Expensive

JACOBSON

There's a famous book in food literature called *Thin Cook, Fat Cook*, and Alex Stratta, who has lost close to 100 pounds during the past two years, is a fat one. He's thin now, but he hasn't lost any of his passion, style, or infallible technique. At his restaurant, the Wynn Grande Dame, one might find Elizabeth Taylor or the Dalai Lama, and Steve Wynn entertains his most important guests here. Stratta's mentor, Alain Ducasse, owns restaurants in Vegas, Paris, and all over the world. The fact that Stratta was a hotel brat also contributes to the international flavors in his cooking. You'll start with too many *amuses*, served in waves—foie gras lollipops and the like—and then progress to seasonal vegetables, fish, and game, dressed with such fancy accoutrements as more foie gras and truffles. A dinner at Alex is fussy, probably the most classically French of the Big Five (Guy Savoy, Joël Robuchon, Picasso, and Twist being the other four). But it's never dull, and Master Sommelier Paolo Barbieri is the best in the business.

MANCINI

Before you even start eating at Alessandro Stratta's inspired Italian spin on classical French cuisine, the ambience of Alex will knock you off your feet. From the moment you walk down the massive marble staircase, inspired by *Hello Dolly*, you'll be transported to a world of pure romance. The outdoor gardens are breathtaking. The polished wood and hanging chandeliers are stunning. And only the most jaded of ladies won't be impressed when they're offered an ornate stool at the side of their chairs, so their purses won't have to touch the ground. Simply put: If you can't get laid after taking your date here, you're better off picking up one of those hooker books they hand out on the Strip (which might be a less expensive option anyway). The food itself is perfect, while Stratta is one of the most down-to-earth guys you'll ever meet. And while Max is busy looking for Liz Taylor or the Dalai Llama, those below retirement age should keep their eyes peeled for one of Stratta's rock-star friends. Tool's Maynard Keenan, for example, has been known to relax here and sip wine from his personal vineyard after helping the chef prepare gnocchi in Alex's more casual sister restaurant Stratta.

CURTAS

Las Vegas' most dramatic dining room is run by one of its hardest working on-premises chefs, whose coming to Las Vegas (in 1998) was as important and influential as any event in the 1990s in raising Las Vegas' fine-dining profile. Alex Stratta's food can best be described as Mediterranean-influenced French with the occasional Italian twist. Sometimes the presentations aren't as inventive or sophisticated as you might expect in a restaurant as beautiful as this, but one taste of his veal sweetbread puff pastry with swiss chard, fresh plums, and toasted almonds, or butter-poached Maine lobster with sweet corn custard, and all is forgiven. As with most wine lists at Wynn/Encore, this one contains page after page of sticker shock. It's not for the faint of heart or wallet, so we recommend ordering the by-the-glass selections, masterfully put together by MS Paolo Barbieri; they're (relatively) reasonable and well-matched to the food.

Author Picks

Sweetbreads with pasta and artichoke (seasonal);
anything foie gras; duck "Apicius"

BARMASA (Strip)

Aria at CityCenter
(877) 230-2742
arialasvegas.com
Wed.-Sun., 5-10:45 p.m.
Very Expensive

CURTAS

The only place to go in Las Vegas for sushi, sashimi, and Japanese food—as long as someone else is paying. The pristine quality of the raw ingredients (most flown in from Japan) is immediately apparent (if you have a yen for such things), and a meal here is an immediate education in the subtleties that comprise a superior Japanese dining experience. Unfortunately, for the Western palate, Japanese food has an elusive quality to it that borders on the invisible. Whether you can appreciate these fine distinctions, and just how flush you're feeling, will determine whether you think paying $15 apiece for toro, or $10 apiece for akamutsu (deep-sea fatty snapper), or $34 for a kegani hairy-crab salad is worth it. The other problem with BARMASA is the cavernous space and informal décor. True Japanese aficionados (and high rollers) will ignore the gymnasium feel of the place and be dazzled by the dancing shrimp, while mere mortals might be happier with more pedestrian choices in this genre.

MANCINI

I have to disagree with John on the décor. Yes, the place is massive and cavernous and the tables are arranged cafeteria-style. But with an arched canopy ceiling, cylindrical light fixtures that descend from it like illuminated raindrops, and a glass wall that exposes the towers of CityCenter, it has an air of ultra-modern simplicity to it. The food is pristine, with fish flown in from Tokyo Bay arriving in the kitchen within 16 hours of being caught. And the chef's intimate knowledge of the Japanese fishing season allows him to offer seasonal specialties you won't find in many other places. But the prices will kill you. Entrance to the semi-private shabu shabu and sukiyaki dining room Shaboo starts at $300 per person. And spending even half of that in the main dining room will likely have you going home hungry.

JACOBSON

When chef Masa Takayama opened Ginza Sushi-Ko in Beverly Hills, circa 1990, he set the dining world on its ear. At approximately $350 per person, the chef kept a notebook of every dish that every guest ate in his eight-seat restaurant to avoid repetition upon their return. Then he relocated to the Time-Warner Building in New York, got a four-star review from the *New York Times*, and became a national celeb. In 2009, he opened a larger version of the place at Aria, but the price and quality didn't waver. The problem is, do you really want to pay several hundred dollars for an impersonal sushi experience and leave hungry? The experience in this Amish-barn-sized place is lost in translation. An exquisite toro nigiri sushi, two pieces at an astonishing $145, explains elegantly why this product is so prized by the Japanese. Is it worth it? Only for the most cultivated palates with disposable incomes.

Author Picks

Toro tartare with caviar; spear squid; octopus in butter;
kanpachi sushi roll

BARTOLOTTA RISTORANTE DI MARE [Strip]   Italian

Wynn Las Vegas
(702) 770-3463
wynnlasvegas.com
5:30-10 p.m., daily
Expensive

MANCINI

On a good weekend, you'll find between 50 and 60 different species of seafood here, and everything was swimming in the Mediterranean 48 hours before it hit your plate. Paul Bartolotta has become such a huge (and generous) purchaser of Italian seafood that chefs on the Italian coast reportedly curse his name for driving up the prices of their local species. And if you dine here, you'll understand their frustration, because the prices at times can be a kick in the gut. But the ingredients alone are worth the cost of admission and the chef's treatment of them is superb. The best bet is to splurge for one of the family-style tasting menus. And if the weather's nice, request one of the cabana tables overlooking the romantic outdoor pool.

CURTAS

A seafood-lover's dream, as long as you have the lira to luxuriate in langoustines and gallinella (sea robin) flown in from 7,000 miles away. No one celebrates the simplicity of ingredients like the Italians, and no one knows this better than Paul Bartolotta, who lavishes his love on seafood with a less-is-more approach. His reputation rests on his reverence for raw materials and a knack for letting great ingredients speak for themselves. Every meal begins when you're shown the catch of the day, but everything is priced by the gram (because Americans are so good at calculating prices by the gram), so unless you have a metric calculator in your head, be prepared for one of those whole branzino or orata adding a cool Benjamin to your bill. Stick with the pastas and other Italian specialties and you'll experience one of America's great restaurants without breaking the bank.

JACOBSON

Paul Bartolotta is from Milwaukee, Wisconsin, a good distance from the Bay of Naples and the Adriatic, places from which he sources the esoteric sea creatures he prepares at his restaurant. If names like astice, spigola, or occhiale mean nothing to you, they will after a meal here, where the bespectacled chef prepares them fresh, in the classic Italian manner. The four-ingredient rule, no more than four ingredients in a dish, is king here. The chef steams, sautés, broils, and salt crusts his fish, then serves them simply. He gives great pasta as well. I'm in love with scampi alla Diavolo, spicy broiled whole shrimp you suck from the shells; agnolotti del plin, tiny pasta pockets with a veal filling drizzled with butter and sage; and fish done alla Palermitana, with capers, tomatoes, and olives. The chef is both a fanatic and a master technician, so expect perfection. At these prices, you'd better get it.

Author Picks

Grilled tiger shrimp; whole roasted wild turbot; grilled cuttlefish; brown-butter tortellini; Branzino alla Palermitana

Palazzo
(702) 607-6300
palazzolasvegas.com
Sun.-Thurs., 5:30-10 p.m.; Fri.-Sat., 5:30-11 p.m.
Expensive

JACOBSON

Wolfgang Puck's Beverly Hills CUT was designed by architect Richard Meier, who also did the Getty Center in Los Angeles, but the décor at this CUT—post-modern, cold as ice, and not done by Meier—is clearly not the draw. (Even WP told me he didn't like it.) But all things considered, CUT is, in my opinion, the best steakhouse in the city. Everything, from the hot potato knishes to the Sherry Yard-inspired desserts, such as a mixed-berry crumble, is fabulous. Puck's team of Spago Beverly Hills Chef Lee Hefter, our own David Robins, and Matt Hurley is the most experienced in the business. I'm a sucker for the bone-marrow flan starter, and these meats, grilled over hardwood and finished on a superheated broiler, are amazing. Pass on the overpriced Japanese Wagyu in favor of a 35-day Dry Aged Prime steak from Nebraska. If you must have Kobe, the Kobe beef short ribs with curried pea purée and Indian spice is good enough to make a PETA member blush with envy.

CURTAS

A dead ringer for the original in Beverly Hills … at least as far as the menu is concerned. Whether you think this is a good or bad thing depends on how much creativity you demand in your super-expensive steakhouses. Everything from the bone-marrow flan to the lamb chops with a mint-cucumber raita has been vetted by the likes of Leo DiCaprio, so you're assured it all passes the celebrity taste test. One thing movie stars must love is having all the raw cuts pristinely presented to the table to stimulate their carnivorous cravings. As good as the beef is, the starters, salads, sides, and seafood will have you dropping your fork. We're partial to the thyme-lavender roasted duck and classic Dover sole and have had equally stunning meals of small plates from the appetizers and sides. None of it's original; all of it's superb. The wine list is aimed at those with more money than imagination.

MANCINI

While I don't think CUT serves the best steak in town (I reserve that honor for Mario Batali's Carnevino), it is unquestionably the overall best steakhouse. That's because Wolfgang Puck and his local crew deconstruct the very notion of what a steakhouse is, stripping bare all the basic elements and reinventing them for the modern world. If that doesn't make sense to you, just stop by the bar one day and order the bone-marrow flan, the oxtail bullion with chive blossoms, chervil and marrow dumplings, or anything else in the appetizer section. Once they've made a believer out of you, make a reservation for the spectacular modern dining room to enjoy a full meal. The décor is amazing and even the futuristic black servers' uniforms are bad-ass. After one meal here, you'll never visit your favorite local steakhouse again without feeling a little disappointed.

Author Picks

Bone-marrow flan; veal tongue with marinated artichokes; Wagyu sliders; Kobe/Wagyu beef tasting; potato knishes

The Top Ten

JOEL ROBUCHON (Strip)

French

MGM Grand
(702) 891-7358
mgmgrand.com
Sun.-Thurs., 5:30-10 p.m.;
Fri.-Sat., 5:30-10:30 p.m.
Very Expensive

MANCINI

If there's one word to describe Robuchon's namesake restaurant, it's "exquisite." The atmosphere is exquisite, with plush seats, ornate chandeliers, and a dining experience that makes you feel like you're eating in one of the most intimate salons in the palace at Versailles. The service is exquisite, with unparalleled touches, like a server who not only guides you through the many bread choices available on the restaurant's bread cart, but then removes your selections to warm them for you before placing them at your table. And the food is exquisite in both taste and presentation. Robuchon and his staff offer the flashiest food in town, expertly blending classic French technique and modern cooking methods. Sure, it's expensive—and if you can afford it, you should splurge for the tasting menu. But the more approachable two-course menu also includes an *amuse-bouche*, selections from the bread cart, and access to the mind-blowing dessert trolley, so you won't go home hungry. As an added bonus, everyone who dines at Robuchon is entitled to complimentary limousine service to and from the restaurant.

CURTAS

Bring money, and an appetite. Because you'll need both to support the ornate, precise, and highly decorative food that earned Monsieur Robuchon "Chef of the Century" status by the Gault Millau Guide in 1997. In case you're wondering, Joël hasn't lost his fastball, mainly because he employs possibly the best relief pitcher in the business, James Beard's Southwest Chef of the Year 2010 Claude Le Tohic. Between them, they create seasonal menus of impeccable provenance, characterized by elaborate intense preparation of everything from cilantro cream and soybeans cooked risotto-style to turbot en cocotte. As pitch-perfect as those provisions are, the mood of the room can sometimes seem too somber—as if you're dining in a cathedral—which, in effect, you are, with prices that are ungodly and a wine list that will make you pray for salvation. Desserts, by perennial James Beard nominee Kamel Guechida, are, like the bread and cheese carts, worth a trip all by themselves.

JACOBSON

Two years ago on Valentine's Day, I ate the tasting menu in this Art Deco dining room, an oasis from the chaos on the MGM casino floor. The first course was composed of buttery pastry wafers, perfectly round, topped with equally round slices of black truffle, little circles lining the plate completely. On top were foie gras shavings. I asked the Maître d' how long it took to plate. He told us that each plate took 20 minutes. That was one course, at a table of four, from a 17-course tasting menu. Just imagine how much effort the entire dinner required. This kind of attention to detail is what makes Joël Robuchon the best French restaurant in this country, though matchless bread and pastry carts certainly contribute to the show. Jamin, his famous Three Star in Paris, had 40 chefs to serve 35 covers, an astonishing ratio. Robuchon, the ultimate perfectionist, would allegedly scrap an entire table's food if one of the dishes came up 30 seconds late on the line.

Author Picks

La Tomate; truffled langoustine with chopped cabbage;
cauliflower cream with caviar; roasted lobster with green curry;
lobster in a sealed cocotte with morels and asparagus

L'ATELIER DE JOEL ROBUCHON [Strip]   French

MGM Grand
(702) 891-7358
mgmgrand.com
Sun.-Thurs., 5:30-10 p.m.;
Fri.-Sat., 5-10:30 p.m.
Very Expensive

CURTAS

L'Atelier (the word means "work-shop") combines an open kitchen surrounded on three sides by a counter with the look of a sleek Japanese sushi bar, from which diners watch a team of intense, almost religious-looking, chefs cook incredible French food served like Spanish tapas by American waiters. The sense of exquisite food being perfectly rendered is palpable when you enter the place, and the joy of L'Atelier is letting your appetite and imagination take flight with some of the tastiest food you will ever encounter. Begin with crisp langoustine fritters served with a smudge of basil pesto. From there the possibilities range from good prosciutto served with toasted tomato bread, ethereal poached kumamoto oysters sitting in their shells in a warm bath of salted butter, to a beautiful piece of sautéed duck liver atop a tiny minced-citrus "gratin." L'Atelier is hands down the favorite everyday restaurant of every chef and foodie in Las Vegas. It's expensive (though far less expensive than its big brother next door), but almost flawless. Every dish highlights what perfectionist chefs—JR ably assisted by Executive Chef Steve Benjamin and Pastry Chef Kamel Guechida—can do with the best ingredients money can buy. The only thing we hate about it is its location deep in the bowels of the always-annoying MGM Grand. If it were easier to get to, we'd eat here once a week.

MANCINI

There's nothing as amazing as watching a world-class cooking staff in action. The teamwork and immaculate attention to detail necessary to churn out picture-perfect versions of every signature dish dozens of times a night is mind-boggling. It's kind of like a well-choreographed dance (or, if you're too macho for that analogy, insert your favorite sports reference instead). Realizing what a great show his staff puts on, Joël Robuchon has made them the centerpiece of L'Atelier. In addition to the show, L'Atelier boasts a modern red and black décor. Where Robuchon's flagship restaurant feels like a French palace, this one is more reminiscent of a Tokyo nightclub. While prices are considerably lower than at the formal restaurant, the place is still expensive. But if you arrive before 6:45, you can get a special three-course $45 L'Unique menu that's probably the most affordable meal of Robuchon's food you're ever going to find.

JACOBSON

W.C. Fields has a wonderful epitaph: "On The Whole, I'd Rather Be in Philadelphia." I feel the same way about L'Atelier, despite the fact that Joël Robuchon at the Mansion, just next door, is the best restaurant in the U.S. This is the master's casual venue and the cooking is symphonic, even if seating, at a 26-seat counter or at tables with tall awkward stools, is less than ideal. Robuchon's resident chef, Steve Benjamin, is a wonder. Here, the idea is tasting portions, inspired by kaiseki, multi-course Japanese dinners. Le jambon, imported prosciutto eaten with crushed tomatoes on toast, is a logical starting point. Les anchois, Spanish anchovies artistically plated with sliced eggplant confit, has to be the best anchovy dish in the world. Among main courses, look for le thon rouge, lightly seared tuna belly with onion rings, or la caille, free-range quail stuffed with foie gras astride Robuchon's potatoes, basically butter stirred with a minimum of potato. A little dab'll do ya.

Author Picks

Le Unique $49 tasting menu (available before 6:45);
roasted quail stuffed with foie gras

PICASSO (Strip)

Bellagio
(702) 693-7223
bellagio.com
Wed.-Mon., 6-9:30 p.m.
Very Expensive

CURTAS

I like everything about this place except the art. It detracts from the food. It's the only restaurant in the world where you could see diners walking around the room and treating it like a mini-museum of the master's works. In the kitchen, the master is Julian Serrano, whose Cal-Ital-Mediterranean cooking has earned him two Michelin stars and a devoted following of foodies, local and international. Take your eyes off the paintings and you'll notice a fine-tuned trademark of Serrano's oeuvre, such as the sweetest Nantucket scallops you'll ever taste and various masterful treatments of foie gras. The wine list, overseen by Master Sommelier Robert Smith, is rich with the varietals of Spain and other Mediterranean climes. For food, wine, and décor of this caliber, the tariff—$95 for three courses; $123 for six, plus an *amuse-bouche* here and a pre-dessert there—is remarkably reasonable.

MANCINI

I first dined at Picasso over a decade ago when I was visiting Las Vegas on vacation. It was intended as the high-class centerpiece of my otherwise middle-class trip and ate up a large portion of my fairly limited budget. At that point in my life, I was lucky if I ate food on this level once a year. It's easy to become slightly jaded by fine dining, so I love to think back to that first visit; I left the restaurant awestruck and considering it worth every hard-earned penny. From being seated under an original Picasso painting to watching one of the best views of the Bellagio fountains available, ambience just doesn't get much better than this. But, of course, the centerpiece was (and remains) the food. Master Chef Julian Serrano combines the cuisine of France and his native Spain in a way that's totally original. And if wine's your thing, his cellar boasts 1,500 different bottles.

JACOBSON

Will success spoil Julian Serrano? I doubt it. Now that he's doing double-duty with his Aria tapas bar, he won't be spending as much time in the kitchen at his flagship. Does this really matter? Probably not much, since he hasn't changed the menu substantially here since opening day during the last century. And the excellent supporting cast, led by Japanese Executive Sous Yoshi, peerless Maître d' Ryland, and the terrific Master Sommelier Robert Smith, is the best in the city. I've eaten more meals here than in any of what I consider Las Vegas' Big Five restaurants and have never been disappointed. Perhaps the cooking has been upstaged by that of Twist, Robuchon, and Savoy, but you always know what you'll be eating: quail salad, medallions of fallow deer, and a glass of PX (Pedro Ximenez), the syrupy Spanish dessert wine, afterwards. The tableaux and sculptures by the master himself are timeless, perhaps even more so than Serrano's time-warp menu.

Author Picks

Roasted pigeon with wild rice risotto;
medallions of fallow deer

The Top Ten

RESTAURANT GUY SAVOY (Strip)   French

Caesars Palace
(702) 731-7110
caesarspalace.com
Wed.-Sun., 5:30-10 p.m.
Very Expensive

MANCINI

Franck Savoy often jokes that I'm the only person in the world who looks as weird as I do he'd even allow to set foot in his restaurant. And I'll admit, I do look a little out of place here. The dining room at Guy Savoy is simple, modern, and elegant—a stark contrast to the flashy ornate opulence of his Paris contemporary Joël Robuchon. And that same distinction applies to the differences in their food. Savoy is clearly a master of modern French cooking. But his cuisine has a deceptive simplicity. The wow factor in such dishes as his truffle and artichoke soup, oysters in ice gelée, crispy sea bass, and butter-roasted sweetbreads, comes from their pristine balance of tastes and perfect rendering by the chef's expert kitchen staff. For a real treat, reserve the kitchen table, where you can see and hear the chefs at work. Or if you really want to splurge, reserve the private Krug Room, where a special menu is paired with offerings from the world-renowned Champagne house.

CURTAS

The most fundamentally French of all of the frog ponds in town, Guy Savoy's food is never less than perfect and always perfect with wine—preferably French. His list is probably the city's best, both in breadth and depth, and it's filled with trophy bottles from Savoy's cellar in Paris, as well as a large selection of reasonably priced new-world producers. Encyclopedia-sized, it's brought to the table with its own stand for your perusal. No matter what you choose, you can depend on Savoy's food being spot-on renditions of the dishes that earned his restaurant three Michelin stars in Paris (it has two here), as well as using the best of American produce. Savoy features no beef in his Parisian original, but he's proud of his tournedos, as well as the American veal proudly plated and served by the top-notch staff. Overseen by Savoy *fils* Franck, the sleek and spare dining room is perfectly lit, has even better acoustics, and would make even Gerard Depardieu look good.

JACOBSON

Some find the design by Paris architect Jean-Pierre Wilmotte on the austere side, but everyone seems to agree that the Krug Champagne room and matchstick sculpture in the bar are impressive. What I like best about Guy Savoy is the seasonal and off-the-menu cooking that is almost impossible to get outside France: aged grouse en cocotte in winter, and in the fall poulet en vessie, chicken in foie gras sauce cooked inside of a pig's bladder. I also like that Chef Savoy has trusted his name to his son. Despite the formal pedigree, this is the friendliest of the haute-French restaurants in Vegas and Franck, Guy's son, is an honest charming host. I can't say the bread cart is up to Robuchon's or the cooking as creative as that of Twist. But overall, this is a place that I don't mind eating in several times a year and the core originals, dishes such as peas all around, oysters en gelée, and that artichoke soup with truffles and parmesan, never fail to make me happy.

> ## Author Picks
>
> Artichoke soup with black truffle and Parmesan cheese; mosaic of milk-fed poularde, foie gras, and artichoke; "peas all around"; "colors of caviar"; oysters en gelée

Mandalay Bay
(702) 632-9300
rmseafood.com
Tues.-Sat., 5:30-10:30 p.m.
Expensive

MANCINI

After Rick Moonen's appearance on season two of "Top Chef Masters," viewers have been flocking to his two-story rm seafood at Mandalay Bay. Most are just happy to dine on sushi, fish & chips, or catfish sloppy Joes in his informal downstairs restaurant. The food there is great if you're just looking for a casual meal, and the ambience is perfect for TV groupies who just want to get the chef to sign their cookbooks (or, at times, body parts). But to really experience Moonen's genius, try the fine dining at rm upstairs. Despite his reputation as one of America's greatest seafood chefs, the diverse menu also features plenty of land-based dishes, like his inspired interpretation of beef tartare, foie gras with sea urchin, a rabbit trio, and a succulent roasted pork belly. And come fall, you may even get to try the venison preparation that caused Vegas-hating moron judge Jay Rayner to question Moonen's commitment to environmental sustainability on the finale of "Top Chef Masters."

JACOBSON

I'm sure Al and John will prattle on about sustainability and all that stuff. I'd rather talk about Adam Sobel and Gerald Chin, the Abbott and Costello of Vegas chefs, who do the bulk of the cooking here. The globetrotting Moonen would rather be fishing on the Copper River in Alaska than cooking in his dining room, but there's no denying this is one of the Ten Best Vegas Restaurants. And I'd rather eat here than almost anywhere else in town. Describing a dish or two seems futile, since the boys tweak the menu constantly and the fish selection changes frequently. But just as an example of what is done, let's define this as refined American seafood molecular gastronomy, with touches of political correctness and environmental sensibility. Got all that? I didn't think so. Oh well, you can always go downstairs to R-Bar and eat a shrimp cocktail, if that's your speed. If shrimp aren't on anyone's endangered lists at the moment.

CURTAS

We'll say this for Rick Moonen, Adam Sobel, and Gerald Chin: They've set a mighty high bar at a mighty reasonable price with their $75 five-course menu at rm upstairs. These three amigos search for the right blend of taste, value, and dazzle factor for their prix-fixe dinner. If you judge the success of such things by plate pirouettes, then you'll find no fault with their marinated tuna atop a pineapple confit, octopus with paper-thin bacon and egg, foie gras à la Japonne with sea urchin croquant (whatever that is). Some of the food seems to be trying too hard, but mostly it works (especially if you're the sort who wants that dazzle with your dinner). The issue we have isn't with the flavors or flawless execution, it's with whether or not the dining-out public needs or wants food this inventive and challenging. In other words, for all its glories, Rick Moonen's flagship might just be too hip for the room. But give credit where it's due: rm upstairs is, by far, the best deal in fine dining on the Las Vegas Strip.

Author Picks

"Steak 'n' potatoes" beef tartare; taramosalata

TWIST BY PIERRE GAGNAIRE [Strip]   French

Mandarin Oriental at CityCenter
(888) 881-9367
mandarinoriental.com
Tues.-Sat., 5:30-10 p.m.
Very Expensive

JACOBSON

I first ate Pierre Gagnaire's cuisine more than 20 years ago when he had a restaurant in St. Etienne, France. There, he dazzled me with the most creative cooking I had ever tasted up to that point in my life. The restaurant eventually went bankrupt, but Gagnaire went on to Three-Star glory in Paris and a worldwide empire. Twist is the most cutting-edge of the Big Five. This isn't just food you've never tasted; it's food you've never imagined. Take, for example, langoustine five ways, a highlight of the tasting menu. Five small dishes arrive with langoustines as their centerpiece: one grilled with avocado, a tartare with Campari turnips and baby greens, one seared with bell pepper and Iberico ham, a mousseline in a Manzanilla sherry butter, and a gelée with kombu and lobster coral. I love the intensely flavored mushroom broth "zezette," French slang for "wacky," the broth redolent of chicken and stocked with vegetable gnocchi. The broth is accompanied by a

Bloody Mary sorbet, ratatouille Bavarois, and a perfectly round codfish croquette that tastes exactly like a Korean fish cake. *Quelle surprise!*

MANCINI

The name of this restaurant says it all: The sometimes insane-sounding, though always delicious, twists Gagnaire puts on his food set him apart from Las Vegas' other Paris masters. Who else would think of offering a side dish of potato ice cream with osetra caviar? And that's one of the chef's simpler concoctions. His appetizers and entrées all contain far too many components to fit on a single plate. They may not be as visually flashy as what you'll get at Robuchon, but their effect on your palate is unparalleled and more often than not will leave you wondering about the kind of mad genius who envisions these combinations. And everything is served up in an intimate, modern, and elegant dining room, designed by Adam Tihany, that offers a spectacular view of the Strip from the Mandarin Oriental's 23rd floor.

CURTAS

If Robuchon is the most elaborate and Savoy the most elegant of Las Vegas' great restaurants, Gagnaire matches them with his restlessly creative cuisine, which can be by turns exhilarating, hyperdelicious, and downright baffling. You don't go to a Gagnaire restaurant looking for a traditional big-deal meal any more than you go to a progressive jazz concert expecting to hear "She'll Be Comin' Round the Mountain." One look at his scallop carpaccio with Campari-rum beet wurtz tells you that you're in the hands of the *enfant terrible* of French cooking. The years haven't dimmed Gagnaire's incessant search for astounding edibles and one taste of his Nebraska sirloin with escargot sauce and venison ice cream provides a window into the intellectual curiosity that drives his talent. As crazy-good and creative as the food is, both the understocked bar and the absurdly priced (and small) wine list fall well below the standards set by the cuisine.

Author Picks

Confucius duck; shellfish "Royale"; never never veal;
langoustines five ways; the whole bleeping menu

Medallions of Fallow Deer at Picasso

Section II

The Rest of the Best

AMERICAN FISH (Strip)

Seafood

Aria at CityCenter
(877) 230-2742
arialasvegas.com
Tues.-Sun., 5-10:30 p.m.
Expensive

CURTAS

It's fairly obvious that when CityCenter was being planned, the restaurateurs were given the mandate to make their menus simpler than their stores in Bellagio. Mina (now with 17 restaurants under his belt) followed the script by making his menu homey (if you can call $36 pieces of fish "homey") and accessible. The conceit here is fish cooked one of four ways: poached in sea water, baked in sea salt, wood grilled and smoked, and "griddled" over cast iron. No trios, no pirouettes on the plate, just solid ingredients respected and cooked with care. American Fish won't send you away swooning, but its something-for-everyone approach exhibits as much passion and pride of product as possible in a corporate restaurant in a behemoth of a hotel. Skip the overpriced wine and concentrate on the excellent classic cocktails from a bar that takes real pride in its gimlets, manhattans, and martinis. The noise level, when this place is busy, is intolerable.

MANCINI

No matter how many Las Vegas restaurants Michael Mina opens (this is his fifth), they never get stale for me. His latest, and best, is his personal spin on a mountain lodge. While the menu has plenty of variety, the showcase kitchen has the four primary stations John describes. It's hard to pick a favorite, but I think the salt preparation is the best of an amazing bunch. And yes, I know a lot of critics (like John) have criticized Mina for the pretentiousness of flying in seawater from Hawaii for the poaching process. But anyone who's ever sampled Las Vegas tap water will be thrilled to know their fish isn't being bathed in that swill. When ordering cocktails, pay special attention to the pre-1940 offerings, the house specialty. I was nearly laughed out of the lounge once (quite justifiably) when I asked for a shot of Jagermeister.

JACOBSON

No one can deny chef/owner Michael Mina is relentlessly creative, but it's an open debate as to whether or not he has too many restaurants in Vegas. American Fish, however, breaks the mold and in many ways is his best effort here. Chef de Cuisine Sven Meade shows influences of his onetime boss, Charlie Trotter. Meade collaborated on the menu with Mina; the result is sheer sophistication. Terrific appetizers include Spanish mackerel with sea beans, radish, and fresh ginger, and South Carolina-style shrimp and grits, elevated to gourmet status with jalapenos and tiny shards of Serrano ham. Japan even rises to the surface in a great Kobe beef and abalone shabu-shabu. Among main dishes, try North American turbot, firm, clean, and penetrating, or griddled cornmeal-crusted rainbow trout with an inspired apple, fennel, and bacon vinaigrette.

Author Picks

Blue prawn baked in sea salt; Spanish mackerel in ginger broth;
Kobe beef and abalone shabu-shabu

The Rest of the Best

AUREOLE (Strip)

French

Mandalay Bay
(702) 632-7401
aureolelv.com
5:30-10:30 p.m., daily
Expensive

CURTAS

The Adam Tihany-designed room is as striking as ever. Nothing about the place seems tired or shopworn. And the food is just about as good as finely tuned French food can be in a restaurant that seats more than 300. Truth be told, that's always been the most remarkable thing about Aureole. Everyone talks about the 40-foot-tall wine tower and the computerized (and expensive) wine list, but what has always distinguished Charlie Palmer's palace is how inventive, sophisticated, and consistent the food has been in a place the size of an Army mess hall. Vincent Pouessel now leads the kitchen brigade here and impresses with his command of everything from agnolotti with morels in tarragon foam to lamb chops to even a treatment of sturgeon that will have

32

Eating Las Vegas

you rethinking this bottom feeder. Cheese lovers, remember: Aureole was the first Strip restaurant to feature a quality carte des fromages. And if great chocolates and desserts are your thing, Pastry Chef Megan Romano still dazzles with superior sweets.

JACOBSON

Nothing exceeds like excess, and Charlie Palmer's signature Vegas outpost has won stars, diamonds, and everything but Megabucks. Everyone who walks though Mandalay Bay peeks in at the four-story Lucite wine tower designed by Adam Tihany. Wine "angels" ascend it with harnesses to retrieve your bottle from the restaurant's 2,000-plus label inventory, and Master Sommelier William Sherer will guide you through and make an appropriate choice. Palmer's heavily reduced guy food by Vincent Pouessel is solid and often brilliant. Skate wings, morels in Parmesan foam, spring-pea ravioli, short ribs and Hudson Valley foie gras stand out on the eclectic French-tinged menu. The best tables are in the Swan Court, at the restaurant's rear by the burbling fountains. And Megan Romano's desserts are the cat's meow. Grab a box of her chocolates on the way out. Taste her blood-orange sorbet and you may not want to leave.

MANCINI

As someone who prefers a stiff martini or a good single-barrel whiskey over a fine bottle of wine, Aureole's world-class wine list is lost on me. So I'll probably never ask one of the gorgeous "wine angels" to fly to the top of the admittedly impressive wine tower to fetch me a pricey bottle of fermented grapes. Because of that, I prefer to enjoy the excellent French cuisine outdoors, away from the restaurant's most eye-catching attraction. Out there, you can relax lakeside and feed the swans, which will excitedly flock to your private patio area if you tempt them with a few crumbs from one of your dinner rolls.

Author Picks

Roasted rack of lamb; cheese cart; roasted skate wing; loin of veal with chanterelles; short ribs

The Rest of the Best

B&B RISTORANTE (Strip)

Italian

Venetian
(702) 266-9977
bandbristorante.com
5-11 p.m., daily
Expensive

JACOBSON

Celebrity is indefinable, but there's no doubt that La Grande Orange, the Food Network's Mario Batali, has it in spades. He's a great cooking teacher and tireless Italian traveler, two reasons why B&B is the best Italian restaurant in Vegas. You might have rabbit porchetta from the Marches in this dark clubby room, or offal-filled (organ-meat) ravioli from Piedmont, depending on which Italian region is being featured. Batali is a fount of knowledge when it comes to obscure dishes and his Corporate Chef, Zach Allen, is masterful at reproducing them. The wine list, done by the other B on the marquee, Joe Bastianich, is mostly about boutique Italian wines; good luck finding one at a reasonable price. The loyal well-drilled staff is knowledgeable and efficient. Even busboys here can describe the pappardelle with stinging nettles and wild boar, or the minted lamb ravioli they call love letters. Looking for spaghetti and meatballs? They'll help you find the nearest Olive Garden, if you insist.

CURTAS

Think of B&B as Babbo-lite—as if Mario Batali had simplified his Greenwich Village flagship to best comport with the middle-brow tastes of the average Vegas conventioneer. Bold flavors rule and the kitchen manages to crank out Vegas' most inventive and interesting pastas. Before you get to your primi piattii, you must first navigate molto Mario's antipasti offerings, which are a joy unto themselves. The

34

warm lamb-tongue salad will make a lamb-tongue lover out of you, as will any of the sliced meats that are either house-made or come from Batali's dad in Seattle. Of the pastas, every one is worth a try, but we couldn't live without the mint pockets with spicy lamb sausage. With the secondi courses, we've always been less impressed. You can almost feel the gas run out of the kitchen after your pastas, and the meat and fish main events never seem to be in the same league as the crazy-good fennel-dusted sweetbreads with sweet-and-sour onions salad or the bucatini alla Amatriciana. As with Carnevino, its sister restaurant down the hall, the Italian wine list is stunningly good and (by Las Vegas standards, anyway) quite fairly priced.

MANCINI

When John says Batali is catering to middle-brow tastes, he's ignoring the respectable selection of offal offerings on B&B's menu. Sure, the basic pastas will knock the socks off of just about everyone. But acknowledging that great Italian cooking grew out of the kitchens of the impoverished, who took advantage of every available piece of meat, the chef works his magic around parts of animals most chefs consider scraps. And it's hard to imagine the typical middle-brow convention-eer really digging into preparations of tongue, tripe, oxtail, beef cheeks, and octopus. But for those who have the guts to try them, they kick ass! (That's one part of the animals that isn't on the menu, by the way.) In fact, one of the greatest moments I've ever had in a restaurant was when I got to share a plate of his lamb's-brain pasta with Batali himself at B&B's bar.

Author Picks

Grilled octopus with borlotti marinade and spicy limoncello; black spaghetti with "nudjua" (Calabrian spicy sausage); beef-cheek ravioli; calamari Sicilian-lifeguard style

Caesars Palace
(702) 731-7110
caesarspalace.com
Sun.-Thurs., 11 a.m.-11 p.m.;
Fri.-Sat., 11 a.m.-midnight
Moderate

CURTAS

Nothing gets our heart racing faster than a bowl of fresh-made Chinese noodles and some soup dumplings. If you're of like mind, we suggest hightailing it here faster than you can say "Boxer Rebellion." Combining classic Chinese peasant and street food with super-cool design, the place looks like it's been draped in a gigantic white, transparent, metal doily, and is meant to resemble either inverted Chinese lace cut into an arabesque pattern or the inside of an inverted bird's nest—all very symbolic and all very Chinese. The food is fabulous, especially the Imperial seafood-soup dumplings (which everyone comes for) and the Chef's Special beef pancake, which resembles a small hamburger enclosed within its own bun. Although the menu is round-eye friendly—with concise descriptions of each dish—make no mistake: This is food by Chinese for Chinese (and other appreciative Asians). Chef Yu Li is straight off the boat, as it were, and he aims for that deep mellow harmony of flavors that this cuisine perfected centuries before all others. Starches and soups are obviously the things to get, but an order of deep-fried duck and braised sea bass in clay pot are perfect ways for round-eyes to round out their meal.

JACOBSON

One enters a corridor of six aquaria filled with goldfish into an arabesque of laser-cut metal, backlit by light-emitting diodes that project a shield of glowing flowers. Designer Yukichi Kawai has copied his own design at the Bird's Nest, the main Olympic Stadium at the Beijing Summer Games. The food here is emphatically not Cantonese, though the menu has various types of dim sum, such as ha gow, noodle-wrapped steamed shrimp, and shu mai filled with pork. Rather, the cuisine is of China's north, a people who cherish cold dishes like pickled cabbage, cucumbers marinated with garlic, and bean curd with chives. Yu Li's house specialties are hand-pulled noodles and Imperial seafood-soup dumplings. His special beef pancake is more like a chewy bun, and be very afraid. It spurts juice when you bite in. What's more, his boiled beef and vegetables in red chili and Chinese spices, a new menu addition, is the hottest dish this side of Hades.

MANCINI

For years, the conventional wisdom has been that for a great noodle house, you need to head to Chinatown. Caesars Palace changed that thinking, however, with the opening of Beijing Noodle No. 9. The noodles are hand-pulled daily in the kitchen, a pretty cool sight if you're lucky enough to arrive while the chef is tossing a fresh batch. You can order them up in any number of preparations, but I recommend the light tomato-and-egg version, which gives them a slight kick, but also allows the noodles themselves to shine through. The menu includes a large selection of soup, beef, seafood, poultry, and vegetable dishes and more than a dozen types of dim sum, dumplings, and Beijing pancakes. And everything can be enjoyed family-style, giving you the chance to try as many things as possible. As for the décor: Forget deciphering Max's attempt to impress you with his vocabulary and just imagine the inside of a giant goldfish bowl!

Author Picks

Noodles with tomato and egg; seafood dumplings; Chef Special noodle with sliced pork; boiled beef and vegetables in red chili

The Rest of the Best

BORDER GRILL (Strip)   Gourmet Mexican

Mandalay Bay
(702) 632-7403
bordergrill.com
Mon.-Thurs., 11:30 a.m.-10 p.m.;
Fri., 11:30 a.m.-11 p.m.;
Sat., 11 a.m.-11 p.m.;
Sun., 11 a.m.-10 p.m.
Moderate

JACOBSON

I first met Susan Feniger and Mary Sue (don't call her Mary) Milliken when they operated the modest City Café on Melrose Avenue in Los Angeles, more than 25 years ago. Later, they opened City Restaurant on La Brea, which had an international menu and a version of Hostess Cupcakes I still jones for. (Simon does one, but nowhere near the one the Too Hot Tamales made at City.) Lots of chefs get credit for this genre: upscale pan-Latino cooking. But these girls just about invented it and I don't care what anyone tells you. I still love to come here, sit by the pool, and sip pomegranate limeade. Food is amazing as ever: green-corn tamales with sour cream and salsa fresca, a ceviche Peruvian-style, chicken adobo quesadillas, the rich tres leches cake. I hate the long walk down an interminable corridor in Mandalay Bay, but some things, let's face it, are worth suffering for.

MANCINI

The location of this restaurant definitely sucks, but the view from the patio of the hot bodies walking to Mandalay's pool area more than makes up for it. As for the food, the Too Hot Tamales and their local staff offer a modern gourmet take on Mexican cuisine that you won't find in many other places. Forget the loads of cheese you're used to and brace

38

yourself to experience brilliant tasty ingredients. And the chefs are passionately dedicated to only using sustainable breeds of seafood, as well as chicken, pork, and beef raised without antibiotics or hormones. Add in the exercise from the long walk to get here and it'll probably be the healthiest Mexican meal of your life.

CURTAS

This is an offshoot of the original in Santa Monica and after dozens of meals in both, we can find no significant differences between the two. The trio of ceviches (Baja-lime-marinated halibut and shrimp with cilantro aioli; Hawaiian-fish-of-the-day with apricot salsa and spicy taro root; Aztec-fish-stuffed avocado with serrano-mint chimichurri) are still our favorite way to start a meal—along with the killer trio of fresh salsas. Just as good are the fish tacos (that'll make you feel like you're staring at an Ensenada sunset), green-corn tamales that taste like Christmas in Monterrey, and cochinita pibil—a huge portion of achiote-marinated pork slow roasted in a banana leaf that puts most Vegas barbecue to shame. About the only thing we don't like about this place is its location. Unless you're a conventioneer at Mandalay Bay, you have a long walk from wherever you park. But Chef Mike Minor's beef-brisket taquitos or chicken chilaquiles make us forget that inconvenience and by the time we're on our third bite of his tres leches cake with passion fruit and prickly pear sauces (or our third shot of top-shelf tequila), the walk doesn't seem so far.

Author Picks

Skirt steak; cochinita pibil; white-corn tamales; all ceviches

The Rest of the Best

BOUCHON (Strip)

French

Venetian
(702) 414-6200
bouchonbistro.com
Mon.-Fri., 7-10:30 a.m.; Sat.-Sun., 8 a.m.-2 p.m.,
5-10 p.m., daily; Oyster bar 3-10 p.m., daily
Moderate

CURTAS

Bouchon is a copy of a copy and has exactly the soul of one. That doesn't mean the food isn't fabulous, but it does mean you'll suffer through metronomic service to experience Thomas Keller's idea of a finely tuned French bistro. Keller's cache still packs 'em in, even though this is probably the hardest restaurant to locate in the entire city. Elevator up to it and walk down a long hall, then be prepared to be bowled

Eating Las Vegas

over by the best bivalves in town. The Dabob Bays and kumamotos always blow us away here, ditto the moules frites au safran. Keller's famous attention to detail has also trained his kitchen crew to turn out faultless renditions of trout Grenobloise, croque madame, and boudin blanc. You won't find better French-bistro food anywhere in America, but there's a coldness to this place that you'll find always leaves you a little bit empty.

MANCINI

There was a time when it bothered me that Thomas Keller opted to bring his middle-tiered Yountville restaurant to Las Vegas, rather than recreating a third incarnation of the French Laundry and Per Se. But unlike the sublime brilliance offered at his super-pricey landmarks, Bouchon is a restaurant you can experience over and over again. Whether you're enjoying a reasonably priced breakfast by the pool or oysters and a beer at the imported zinc bar, this is quite simply the best rendition of a French bistro you'll find anywhere.

JACOBSON

Chef Thomas Keller has been on Charlie Rose and in every national magazine except *Scientific American*. Unlike Wolfie, he's homegrown, and unlike Emeril, he's relatively sublimated. The Adam Tihany design at his Vegas bistro really will make you think you're in Paris, with its tiles and a raw bar straight out of La Belle Epoque. Keller doesn't get fancy here, as he does in his signature restaurant, Napa Valley's French Laundry. I like to come here for the city's best breakfast; flaky croissants and the best pastries around are made in the attached bakery. Almost all foods are sourced from boutique producers. Lamb is from a special purveyor in Pennsylvania, butter is from Vermont, et cetera. Amazing rillettes of salmon are served in a mason jar. Local French chefs come for steak frites, just like they'd get on the Rue Mouffetard.

Author Picks

Moles au safran; chicken and waffles (brunch only);
trout almandine; salmon rillettes in a jar; all pastries

Mandalay Bay
(702) 632-9364
mandalaybay.com
Sun.-Thurs., 11 a.m.-11 p.m.;
Fri.-Sat., 11-1 a.m.
Inexpensive

MANCINI

This is where the gourmet-burger explosion began. Master French chef Hubert Keller was skeptical when he was asked by Mandalay Bay executives to create a hamburger restaurant they were planning for their new shopping mall. But when he finally agreed to take it on, he totally reinvented the concept—and other world-class chefs have been scrambling to imitate him ever since. So while the idea of building your own gourmet hamburger has become commonplace these days, there's no better place to do it than here. The signature burger is the "Rossini": an American Wagyu beef patty topped with fresh-shaved truffles and foie gras offered for $60. I've always believed that grinding up Wagyu beef into hamburger is a waste and it's a little too fatty to combine with fatty duck liver. So I recommend using a leaner buffalo burger as the base instead. And you can save about $25 if you substitute truffle sauce for fresh-shaved black ones.

CURTAS

Fresh ground meat—either Black Angus or Nature Source (our favorite), lightly molded, grilled right, and served on a very fresh bun, with a great beer selection—what more do you need for a perfect burger experience? BB predates the burger mania that's been sweeping the country for several years now, but super-chef Hubert Keller put all of his considerable, sophisticated, and tasty chops into designing this simple sandwich and one bite reveals just why he's revered as a master in the cooking world. There's also choices, like American Kobe (Wagyu) that's not worth it and Colorado lamb that is. A whole slew of toppings are offered—everything from half a lobster to peanut butter and jelly, but a simple Nature Source patty with your favorite cheese is really all you need. Very popular, so go early or late to be guaranteed immediate seating.

JACOBSON

"Give the people what they want," comedian Red Skelton quipped, as he viewed the massive turnout at hated Paramount studio head Harry Cohn's funeral, "and they'll turn out for it." What the people want here is cheeseburgers. Americans can't seem to get enough of them, so the crowd comes to Hubert Keller's seminal upscale joint, which launched the burger craze in Vegas. Is Burger Bar, which grinds meat fresh daily, though hardly to order, really better than the places that sprang from it as Athena sprang from the forehead of Zeus? We're speaking about a host of places: KGB, BLT, every acronym except the INS. The answer, in a word, is no. Still, Burger Bar can be very good, and was our first. The wait, however, is often as long as it is at Slidin' Thru, our first food truck that doesn't just specialize in tacos. Please forgive me my sentiments, but who the hell cares? These are burgers, frevvinsakes.

Author Picks

Buffalo burger with foie gras and truffle sauce; Nature Source burger; Angus cheeseburger; sweet potato fries

The Rest of the Best

CARNEVINO (Strip)

Italian Steakhouse

Palazzo
(702) 789-4141
carnevino.com
5-11 p.m., daily; Taverna, 12-mid.
Expensive

CURTAS

The best steak in town? The answer is simple. If you're a connoisseur of beef, order one of the six- to eight-month-old dry-aged beauties from Molto Mario's Italian steakhouse in the Palazzo. Think 30 days is "aged"? Those are for vegans. Sixty days seems like an old piece of beef to you? A mere tyke. The last one of these ancient porterhouses we had was 260-plus days old and tasted like beef from another planet. The texture is almost ham-like, the flavor like steak infused with some vague subtle essence of blue cheese. You know you're eating steer muscle, but it's beef that has transcended its humble roots and metamorphosed into something ethereal—earthy, funky, silky, and soft—with an umami depth charge that lasts a full five minutes after you've swallowed a morsel. These steaks alone would qualify Carnevino for our top spot, but it also features Batali's boffo pastas and Italian specialties, most of which take a back seat to none in town. Combine all of this with one of the best Italian wine lists on the planet and you have the recipe for Vegas' greatest steakhouse.

MANCINI

I have no problem spending three figures a head for a meal from time to time. But when I do, I usually expect numerous courses of exquisitely prepared cuisine—not a single piece of beef. So I've never been able to justify shelling out for the uber-aged "riserva" that John raves about. And I've never had the balls to ask someone in the Batali organization to comp me one. But that's just fine with me. Because the standard steaks here are the finest steaks I've ever eaten in my life! Dry-aged for an already amazing six to eight months, they're then crusted with sea salt, black pepper, and fresh rosemary and charred to create a crispy outer layer surrounding the succulent beef. And as a bonus, you can afford to precede them with some of Mario Batali's classic appetizers from his various other restaurants. Among those, I recommend the ricotta and egg ravioli and the succulent grilled octopus!

JACOBSON

Initially, I thought to exclude Carnevino, but I came to my senses. I don't agree with John about the ultra-aged beef, but Adam Perry Lang is a fabulous butcher, so the steaks are generally impeccable, and the chef here does make the best salumi this side of Bologna. What I don't like are the usurious prices and that goes double for what I'd call a greedy wine list. I think Mario Batali has done more for Italian food in America than da Vinci did for the Renaissance, but the idea of paying nearly twenty dollars for one large egg-stuffed ravioli makes me think I'll never be buried in a Jewish cemetery if I commit the sin of buying it retail. They do, however, keep these incredible spicy cheese straws at the bar, so occasionally I sneak in and eat a couple for free. I eat here often, actually, whenever I get a mixed group who can't make up their minds whether to do steak or Italian. But I'd rather fress at B&B.

Author Picks

Any steak in the house; "riserva" porterhouse; house-cured duck pastrami; American dry-aged bone-in rib eye

The Rest of the Best

CHINA MAMA (Spring Mtn.)   Chinese

see map 1, page 147
3420 S. Jones Blvd.
(702) 873-1977
11 a.m.-10:30 p.m., daily
Inexpensive

MANCINI

It may have once served as a
bank, but from the outside this
place looks like a converted drive-
thru dry cleaner to me. And while
the interior's a step up, it won't impress anyone. The food, however,
is both amazing and amazingly
inexpensive! The two separate
four-page menus offer a few familiar dishes like chow mein and fried
rice. But for most Americans, they'll be an education in how diverse
Chinese cuisine really is. China Mama has everything from a hot pot of
lamb and vegetables in Szechuan sauce to shredded pork tripe with
pickled mustard. And the pastry section is the perfect place to learn
about dim sum—starting with the incredible steamed juicy pork buns.
I'm not an L.A. rat like Max, so I can't comment on Vegas' Chinese food
versus California's San Gabriel Valley. But I do know the Chinese food in
Vegas generally sucks, and China Mama offers food worthy of New York
or San Francisco's Chinatowns.

JACOBSON

This restaurant is included in our list almost by default, because pick-
ings are slim for Chinese-food fanatics east of Rosemead Boulevard in
the San Gabriel Valley. The specialty is xiao loong bao, eight-to-an-or-
der steamed dumplings from Shanghai that squirt juice when pierced.
The restaurant does the best job of them of anywhere in Vegas, thanks
to a fine fatty pork filling and reasonably tender dough. Because of
that, it's worth it to fade the sterile atmosphere and clumsy service. At

least the servers feign being friendly, more than I can say for most Chinese restaurants with reasonably authentic food that cater to a mostly Asian clientele. Cold dishes are generally dependable here, such as wine chicken or five-spice beef, and the noodle dishes, especially dan dan min, sort of Bolognese, Chinese-style, are at the same level as the dumplings.

CURTAS

"You no like, round eye," are words every lover of good Chinese food must occasionally fight through to get the good stuff. Thankfully, the menu here is entirely in English and the staff (despite their spotty command of same) is always friendly, helpful, and accommodating. Vegas' best off-Strip Chinese is a must for lovers of dumplings, potstickers, pork buns, or Chinese noodles, plus a very good all-around Chinese restaurant. Located in an old bank space on Jones just off Spring Mountain Road, this is Shanghai-noodle cuisine at its best. The things to get are listed under "pastry" and include the soup dumplings known as steamed juicy pork bun (P23 on the menu), pan-fried potsticker (gyoza P27), pan-friend shrimp and green nira (leek) pillow (P31), and the boiled shrimp and greed (sic) nira dumpling (P32). There's also the kung pao cabbage (H93), sliced fish in hot chili sauce (H63), chicken with pickle chili sauce (H50), and the not-to-be-missed flambéed chitlins (H23). Don't miss the lamb with cumin, either.

Author Picks

Lamb with cumin; crispy orange beef; Szechuan fish; shao loong bao (little dragon dumplings)

The Rest of the Best

Paris Las Vegas
(702) 948-6937
eiffeltowerrestaurant.com
Sun.-Thurs., 11:30 a.m.-2:30 p.m.,
5-10:15 p.m.;
Fri.-Sat., 11:30 a.m.-2:30 p.m.,
5-10:45 p.m.
Expensive

JACOBSON

Korean-born Chicago-reared Joung Sohn is flat-out the best woman chef on the Strip. True, she's doing dishes created by her mentor Jean Joho, the Lettuce Entertain You chef/partner who created Eiffel Tower in the image of Everest, his Chicago French restaurant. But the food rivals that of Alex, Savoy, Picasso, even Joël Robuchon. We tend to overlook it, because it caters to mainly tourists, but it has the complete package: window tables peering out onto the Bellagio fountains; beef Wellington, a dish found nowhere else on the Strip; a great cocktail program; a Sunday brunch for locals; and a staff that has been on the job since the restaurant opened. Start with a trio of *amuses*, like smoked salmon on toast points, mushroom strudel, and a tiny thimble of soup, then do Sohn's sautéed foie gras with Bing cherries. Don't eat all of a signature pistachio soufflé for dessert, even if it's the best soufflé in Vegas.

CURTAS

Simply put: carefully rendered French-bistro food, at haute-cuisine prices, served amidst a spectacular setting, accompanied by a wine list that will require a pacemaker adjustment. Everything is satisfying, but overall, it's hardly the kind of grand-luxe food experience you'd expect from the setting or Jean Joho's reputation. This place isn't really about the food, which is just fine with its tourist clientele, who are there for the experience. On that level, the restaurant delivers. But on purely gastronomic terms, culinary expectations are raised above what the kitchen is actually turning out. Adventurous epicureans—those looking for food competing with the likes of Alex, Joël Robuchon, et al.—will be sorely disappointed, but for someone who may never get a taste of the real Paris (and maybe doesn't even want one) and would like to try an unintimidating dose of decent Gallic grub amidst the awesome backdrop of the Las Vegas Strip, the Eiffel Tower Restaurant will fit like a fake beret. And when you consider the spectacular setting (looking down on the Bellagio fountains), perhaps the prices aren't so out of line after all.

MANCINI

Once again, John's snobbery is showing. Who else would refer to dishes like bleu-cheese soufflé pudding with walnuts and pecan, or seared foie gras with braised Bing cherries and Alsace spice cake, as "bistro food?" Yes, the menu leans toward the accessible. The chef wisely realizes that most of his customers don't know his name. This restaurant is a throwback to the days before celebrity chefs of Joho's status invaded Las Vegas. It's simply an old-school "nice restaurant," where you don't have to be embarrassed about asking the tuxedo-clad staff to explain the menu. You can just sit back and enjoy the brilliant view and the romance. (If you're planning to pop the question, call ahead and ask about one of the many engagement packages.) And most customers prefer something simple, like the impeccably prepared rack of lamb with tarragon jus and tomato tart. But "adventurous epicureans" who take the time to look will find a handful of mind-blowing pieces of haute cuisine scattered throughout the menu.

Author Picks

Foie gras with braised Bing cherries and Alsace spice cake; pheasant breast with wild-berry risotto; Beef Wellington; baked herb vegetable crêpe

The Rest of the Best

JULIAN SERRANO (Strip)   Tapas

Aria at CityCenter
(877) 230-2742
arialasvegas.com
11 a.m.-10:45 p.m., daily
Moderate

MANCINI

First things first: Let's make sure you can say the name of Las Vegas' best tapas restaurant. The eponymous undertaking of our town's finest Spanish chef is, like the man himself, pronounced HOO-lee-ahn. (Serrano is pronounced the way it looks.) Now that that's out of the way, call Aria and make a reservation in advance, because this restaurant is packed on most evenings. And with the mastermind behind the fine-dining restaurant Picasso creating affordable delicious tapas, it's no surprise. Some of the menu's best dishes include the stuffed dates, potatoes with spicy tomatoes and aioli sauce, and paquillo peppers stuffed with goat cheese. And while I agree with John that the paella would be better if it were crispier, I still believe the Valencia version, made with chicken, rabbit, chorizo, and vegetables, is a must-try dish.

JACOBSON

Lots of restaurants around town pretend to serve tapas, but only one of them delivers. I've eaten here almost 10 times now, probably more than anywhere else since this restaurant opened, and have never been disappointed. Sure, I'd like the paellas better if they were finished in a wood oven, but they're hand-stirred and stocked with authentic products, easily the best in town. Croquetas, fried cylinders of chicken puréed in Bechamel, actually do melt in the mouth. Jamon Serrano, a distinction not involved with the chef, is the world's best ham, and super-category pata negra, which is ham cured from black-foot pigs that eat nothing but acorns, is a life-changing experience. Padron peppers are a must here, blackened around the edges and dusted with sea salt. And, of course, there's the ultimate Spanish bar dish, tortilla Española, a potato-and-egg omelet served in wedges, like on every bartop from San Sebastian to Seville. We finally have the Spanish restaurant we deserve, a World Cup we can engrave the name Las Vegas on. Bravo, Juli.

CURTAS

One of the great things about Julian Serrano is that it's is open for lunch, so you can graze and indulge until your heart's content without battling the crowds that flock here for dinner. This sprawling place—adjacent to Aria's front desk—became Vegas' best Spanish restaurant the minute it opened. About the only thing on the menu we're not keen on is the paella (not crusty or smoky enough), but the rest of the menu is full of traditional and modern tapas that will have everyone at the table battling for the last bite. Don't miss Serrano's molecular tuna with raspberry, crab gazpacho, deconstructed fish stew, or the silky crema Catalana. Wash it all down with one of Desi Echavarrie's super sherries and you'll feel like fighting a bull—or at least ordering another plate of jamon de bellota de pata negra.

Author Picks

Brava potatoes; crema Catalana; chicken croquettes;
anything but the paella

The Rest of the Best

51

LE CIRQUE (Strip)

Contemporary

Bellagio
(702) 693-8100
bellagio.com
Tue.-Sun., 5:30-10 p.m.
Expensive

JACOBSON

Sirio Maccioni was talked into bringing his seminal New York temple of gastronomy to Las Vegas by his former employee Elizabeth Blau, a principal of Simon and Society. I like to call his son, Mario, the casual dauphin, the accidental restaurateur. The tall suave Mario looks as if he belongs at Sotheby's, auctioning off rich-people's belongings, not hosting a restaurant. But as such, there's no one better in Las Vegas. He's to the manner born and his demeanor reflects that. Le Cirque has had many chefs in the last decade, but the current one, the Alsatian David Werly trained at the Three Star Auberge de L'Ill in France, has one of the most flawless techniques of any Las Vegas chef. The circus-tent décor may once have been cute, but it's as out of date as Dover sole in

Eating Las Vegas

a parchment bag. At least Werly has the good sense to offer a modern and a contemporary menu, both of which are executed flawlessly.

MANCINI

Justifiable or not, New York's Le Cirque had a pretty tumultuous decade in the 2000s. But its Las Vegas counterpart has been going strong since Bellagio opened in 1998. Its tent-like interior is one of the most beautiful dining rooms in town. And while the chefs have changed over the years, the cuisine has remained consistently exceptional. David Werly has been helming the kitchen since 2007, and his menu is split between "classics" like a rabbit symphony of loin, leg, and ravioli, and "contemporary" choices such as honey duck magret with pink praline and coco nibs and apricot & honey coulis. And if you happen to be in town for the holidays, the chef consistently puts out one of the most extravagant Christmas dinners in town.

CURTAS

Everyone seems to look and feel good inside this Adam Tihany-designed jewel box in Bellagio. Only 65 seats, it has aged remarkably well over the past 12 years, and David Werly's cooking is one of the reasons why. His "contemporary" menu, featuring such avant-garde eats as sweetbreads with licorice-prune compote and foie gras with gewürztraminer jelly, has earned it a Michelin Star, and the service staff, most of whom have been with the restaurant since it opened, remains one of the best in the business. Sommelier of the Year (2009) Frederic Montandon oversees a list that skews heavily toward French (it fits the food, after all), but is remarkably well-priced for such a swanky joint. You come to Le Cirque because it's an iconic American restaurant. You'll come back because it treats you so well. P.S. Always save room for the blizzard of desserts that seem to hit every table.

Author Picks

Truffle risotto; rabbit with Riesling; Yuzu-glazed duck with turnips; anything with black or white truffles or with foie

The Rest of the Best

LOS ANTOJOS (Southeast)

Mexican

see map 3, page 149
2520 S. Eastern Avenue
(702) 457-3505
Wed.-Mon., 10 a.m.-10 p.m.;
Tues., 9 a.m.-2 p.m.
Inexpensive

CURTAS

The name roughly translates into "the cravings," and it's a fitting title. The south-of-the-border folks (and more than a few gringos) who love this hole in the wall do so for good reason—the tacos suadero, the consommé loco, the huarache, the alambre, the al pastor, the adobo, the corn tortillas, the chicken mole, and the carne asada taste just like they do in Mexico City! As for that consommé loco, the rich chicken broth is full of shredded chicken, loaded with fresh cilantro, and becomes instantly addictive from the first bite. The chipotle and tomatillo-based salsa verde are world-beaters too. This is a family-run operation, with matriarch Carmen Ruiz running the kitchen and son Francesco Martinez working the (tiny) front of the house. She makes everything from scratch (including a magnificent dark mole), and the always-busy kitchen occupies about 75% of the restaurant's space—giving you an idea how seriously they take the cooking of their homeland. As for the restaurant proper, it seats about 20 happy souls at a time and by 12:15 p.m. every day, a line snakes through it with people of all stripes waiting to place their orders for the best Mexican food in town. Cash only.

JACOBSON

What's a dive largely patronized by blue-collar day laborers where seating is elbow-to-elbow, the best dishes written in Spanish on the wall are often sold out, and the Chilangos (natives of Mexico City) who

54

own the joint barely communicate with Anglos doing in this august company? Elementary, my dear Watson. This is the best Mexican food in town or, for that matter, until you get to the outskirts of Los Angeles. Consommé loco, a chicken-rice soup simmered with cilantro and onions, is as elegant a broth as you'd get in a Louis XV dining salon, while pambazo, baked potatoes with sausage, lettuce, cream, and Mexican cheese, is shot through with Third World animal funk. On weekends, there's the tripe-soup menudo, a legendary hangover cure, and pozole blanco, a hominy stew accompanied by lettuce, radish, and tomato. Then there's the End of Days, gordita with chicharron, a deep-fried corn cake split open and stuffed with fried pork skins. Anyone for an angioplasty?

MANCINI

This is the kind of ethnic hole-in-the-wall dive that Max lives for. But when a snob like John also began raving to me about it, I decided to pay it some attention. And I'm glad I did! While this town has always boasted a handful of good Mexican-fusion places, authentic south-of-the-border cuisine has never been one of its strong points. But Los Antojos has everything you could want, from huaraches and tlacoyos to quesadillas and eight types of tacos, including tongue. Sure, the place isn't glamorous—with cramped tables, homemade photos of the food on the walls, and coin-operated gumball machines. But these people can cook, which might explain why it's always packed with Mexicans looking for a taste of home!

Author Picks

Consommé loco; gordita chicharron; chile relleno

The Rest of the Best

LOTUS OF SIAM (East)

Thai

see map 1. page 147
953 E. Sahara Avenue
(702) 735-3033
saipinchutima.com
Mon.-Fri., 11:30 a.m.-2:30 p.m.,
5:30-9:30 p.m.
(till 10 p.m. on Fri.):
Sat.-Sun., 5:30-10 p.m.
Moderate

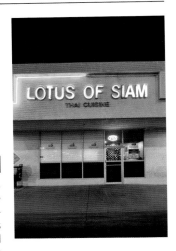

MANCINI

Sure, you've read about Lotus of Siam in other guide books. The restaurant has an ongoing love affair with the national food press that's lasted over a decade. And yes, it's that good, particularly if you ask the waiter to show you the northern Thai menu that offers some of the kitchen's best selections. But if that article you read about the place hasn't already warned you, you should also brace yourself for your visit to one of the most colorful shopping centers in Las Vegas. The seedy-but-safe Commercial Center that houses Lotus is also home to an alternative theater company, an S&M shop, several gay bars, a gay and lesbian center, a gay spa, and several swingers clubs featuring on-premises public sex. So if you want to act out any of your "what happens in Vegas" fantasies after dinner, they're all just a short walk through the parking lot!

JACOBSON

Perhaps Lotus has been overhyped; ever since blowhard Jonathan Gold of the *L.A. Weekly* called it "the best Thai restaurant in the United States," every journo from Bar Harbor to the Aleutians has written an article about the place. Now that it's expanded into a larger space, the restaurant has lost some of its charm, as well. But it's still wonderful, and Saipin Chutima's northern and eastern Thai specialties are easily the most interesting Thai food around, including Los Angeles, which is heavily Thai. (In L.A., try the fiery southern Thai fare at Jitlada in Hollywood.) I never come here without eating nam kao tod, crispy rice salad laced with bits of Thai sausage, lemon grass, and fried peanut, or the khao soi, a Burmese dish consisting of egg noodles, coconut curry, and meltingly tender short ribs (an additional $10 and worth it). The charbroiled beef called nua man tok, the charbroiled beef liver, and Issan sausage, the grainy country Thai sausage that you eat taco-style in the hollow of a cabbage leaf, almost justify Gold's metaphors.

CURTAS

In no other Thai restaurant in town can you find the variety and freshness and vivid flavors put forth by this kitchen on a daily basis. (Those who judge Lotus by its lunch buffet are missing the whole point of the restaurant.) The point of Lotus is the northern and Issan specialties (all in English on the menu), done the way Saipin Chutima's mother taught her and well enough to garner Chutima two James Beard Award nominations (warning: Gringos should avoid asking for anything "Bangkok hot"). Pair these dishes with the extraordinary Rieslings that make up one of the best German lists in the country and you have an experience that Jonathan Gold (the Pulitzer Prize-winning author) calls the best Thai food in the country. We haven't been to every Thai restaurant in the country, but we tend to agree with him, especially when we're lingering over bites of Issan sour sausage, koi soi (raw beef with chiles), or Chutimas' definitive northern Thai curries.

Author Picks

Sai oua; mangos with sticky rice;
khao soi (raw beef dusted with chilies)

The Rest of the Best

M&M SOUL FOOD CAFE (West)   Southern Soul/Barbeque

see map 1. page 147
3923 W. Charleston Blvd.
(702) 453-7685
mmsoulfoodcafe.com
7 a.m.-8 p.m., daily
Inexpensive

JACOBSON

When it comes to barbecue, Southern cooking, or soul food, Vegas is not, let's face it, Kansas City, Memphis, or Savannah. But I confess a weakness for the smothered chicken at Kathy's Southern Cooking on Mountain Vista in Henderson, and Memphis Championship Barbecue is occasionally brilliant as well, usually right after pit master Mike Mills has come to town. For all-around dependability, however, my vote goes to M&M Soul Food. The atmo has all the charm of a hospital cafeteria and the servers, mainly young women, won't be on a runway real soon. Still, the sweet fragrant corncakes that come with your order, gumbo stocked with crab, sausage, and chicken on the bone, and side dishes like collard greens, red beans and rice, or mac 'n' cheese are amazing. And the main dishes, especially fall-apart-tender oxtails, fried chicken with shatteringly crisp crust, and correctly crunchy catfish, show why this enduringly American genre deserves front-page consideration.

CURTAS

Some might argue a soul-food restaurant belongs in our Top 50 about as much as Mr. Bojangles does in *Swan Lake*. But this nondescript lunch counter at the corner of West Charleston and Valley View puts forth superb fried chicken and waffles, cornbread, collard greens, corned-beef hash, and decent enough barbecued ribs to make you think you're almost in Mississippi. Other don't-miss items include the oxtails in special "gravy," good meatloaf, and a respectable gumbo. There's also very sweet iced tea and lemonade—another indication you're in soul-food land—as is the modest décor (it could use a facelift, but what's the point?) and the very modest prices that keep this place humming along with a steady stream of regulars. You'll have a hard time spending more than $40 for two people here. Nothing very fancy goes on, but all of it tastes like it's made with love just seconds before it hits your table. That's because it is.

MANCINI

As with any good ethnic restaurant, I often find myself the only Caucasian in M&M. That's fine with me, because the place has a real sense of community that always makes me feel at home. I've never had a meal here without at least one of the cheerful waitresses asking my name, and the last time I was here for lunch, former heavyweight champ Zab Judah was posing for pictures with the super-friendly staff. I'll admit the lack of racial diversity once caused me to do a double-take when a waiter walked up to me and mumbled, "Cracker?" But I soon realized he was just asking if I wanted crackers with my delicious gumbo. (Which, BTW, is only available on Fridays, Saturdays, and Sundays.) While it's easy to get so engulfed in the rich heavy entrées, if you don't leave room for dessert, that would be a mistake. Because the banana pudding is probably the best dish in Las Vegas priced below $3.

Author Picks
Fried chicken; crab and chicken gumbo; banana pudding

The Rest of the Best

MARCHE BACCHUS (West)

French Bistro

see map 2, page 148
2620 Regatta Drive #106
(702) 804-8008
marchebacchus.com
Mon.-Sat., 11 a.m.-4:30 p.m.; Sun. 10 a.m.-4:30 p.m.;
Mon.-Sun., 5:30-9:30 p.m.; Fri.-Sat., 5:30-10 p.m.
Moderate

CURTAS

Tucked away in a hard-to-find shopping plaza in Desert Shores is Las Vegas' best bistro-cum-wine-bar. Hugely popular with locals, the French-infused fare of Chef Jean-Paul Labadie is as wine-friendly as cuisine gets and goes great with the bottle you pick out from the tiny but well-stocked adjacent wine store. Those $10 markups on all bottles are the big draw and for that we can excuse a kitchen whose reach sometimes exceeds its grasp. For lunch, everyone gets the Croque Monsieur (grilled ham-and-cheese sandwich), although we're partial to the poulet with frites, mussels, and salad niçoise. For dinner, start with the soup a l'oignon and stick with standards, such as Idaho trout, lobster pot pie, or excellent burger, and you won't be disappointed. No matter what the savory course, the highlight of everyone's table is always the croissant bread pudding. They call it "traditional" on the menu, but you'll find it ethereal.

JACOBSON

Where do famous chefs go when they want to socialize and unwind? Many, especially ones with French accents, come to this bucolic lake terrace, now run by Jeff and Rhonda Wyatt, who took the place over in 2007 from founder Gregoire Verge. The Gallic charm remains in spite of the fact that the French-named chef, Jean-Paul Labadie, is Puerto Rican. This is still a wine shop specializing in boutique and high-quality wines, but they have served French foods, like charcuterie and imported cheese, from the beginning. Labadie cooks holdovers from his days with Emeril: pasta jambalaya with andouille sausage, lobster pot pie, and even pan-roasted Idaho trout, to go along with the croque Monsieur and filet mignon with shallot confit. And the wine selection and liberal corkage-fee policy mean the Frenchies, most of whom still have maman's lunch money from lycée, continue to storm the Bastille. Watching the ducks float peacefully by on the man-made lake must be torture for these men, who would rather be sautéing their livers.

MANCINI

There's no restaurant in Las Vegas that feels less like Las Vegas than Marché Bacchus. Tucked away on a man-made lake on the northwest side of town, this is the best place in the valley for a casual lunch on a beautiful spring or fall afternoon. Kids feed the ducks while parents casually nibble on charcuterie and cheese and some of the most reasonably priced wine in town. (Given the prices and selection, even I play wine connoisseur here.) And after several changes in chefs over the past few years, Emeril Lagasse disciple Jean Paul Labadie's French-bistro-inspired menu is a step above those of his predecessors.

Author Picks

Moules frites; bread pudding; charcuterie, and cheese platters

The Rest of the Best

MONTA (West)

see map 1, page 147
5030 Spring Mtn. Road
(702) 367-4600
11:30 a.m.-11 p.m. daily
Inexpensive

JACOBSON

Monta is the best ramen bar I've eaten in since I left Japan in the mid-'80s. Top Ramen debuted in this country during the Vietnam era and quickly became part of the American food landscape. This represents a quantum leap from the MSG-infused packages of dried noodles most of us know as ramen, though. The word is a Japanese pronunciation of the Chinese "la min," or hand-pulled noodles. This tiny place seats at most 20, usually local Japanese or chefs on break, and the menu cuts straight to it. Tonkotsu ramen (pork-bone) come in a milk-white broth, which gets its intense flavor from slow-roasted pork bones. Miso ramen get their clear-broth flavor from bean paste. Choose toppings from a short list: sweet corn, hard-boiled egg, or roast pork in fine fatty slices that melt into the broth like guanciale melts into the sauce in an Amatriciana.

CURTAS

Monta, with its 10-item menu and 26 seats, proves less is more when it comes to restaurant menus. What it serves more of and better than any restaurant in town is ramen—the noodle soup Japan has been going crazy for since the end of WW II. The words "noodle soup" don't usually get an American's heart racing, but the Japanese put a finer point on these things than anyone (save the French) and from your first spoonful, you'll understand what all the shouting is about. Shouting (silently, with joy) is what you'll be doing as the chashu (roasted

Eating Las Vegas

pork) in your bowl melts in your mouth. As you'll be when you sip the tonkotsu broth that simmers for hours to extract every bit of goodness from its base ingredient, or the nutty, sweet, heartier, and thicker miso ramen. A few rice bowls topped with kimuchee, corn, or the ethereal poached eggs and the best gyoza (steamed, then fried, dumplings) in town complete a menu that's a study in simplistic perfection. Monta is the Raku of noodle soups, and one more tiny, but significant, notch on a Las Vegas foodie's belt.

MANCINI

No restaurant in Las Vegas is a better example of the spirit of this book than Monta, because it speaks to each of the three authors in very different ways, yet still impresses the hell out of each of us. For me, Monta represents the type of restaurant that encouraged my early life as a wannabe foodie in New York and is a perfect place to recommend to the young aspiring connoisseurs who inspire my writing. In other words, it's dirt cheap. The food is incredibly accessible, but still has a hint of being slightly exotic. And the room is cozy enough to impress a date, yet comfy enough to take some friends after a late night of drinking. In many ways, it's my dream restaurant. At the same time, it's an ethnic eatery offering a product authentic enough to impresses Max, and the immaculate attention to quality ingredients and preparation that John loves about super-fine dining. Who says one restaurant can't be all things to all people?

Author Picks

Any of the three ramens, kimuchee rice bowl, gyoza dumplings

MOZEN BISTRO [Strip]

Pan-Asian

Mandarin Oriental at CityCenter
(888) 881-9367
mandarinoriental.com
6:30-11 a.m., 11:30 a.m.-2:30 p.m., 6-10 p.m., daily
Moderate

MANCINI

The Mandarin Oriental hotel chain delivers an unparalleled level of luxury and service. And the Las Vegas Mandarin's lack of gaming and position in a far corner of CityCenter leaves it relatively free of curious sightseers, allowing the staff to treat everyone who walks through the door like royalty, whether they're guests or not. So while the resort's flagship restaurant Twist, by world-renowned master Pierre Gagnaire, gets most of the attention here, don't overlook its more casual third-floor sister restaurant. Chef Shawn Armstrong serves up breakfast, lunch, and dinner, drawing heavily on his encyclopedic knowledge of various Asian cuisines. (I personally don't know of anywhere else in town where you can get stingray with spicy Singapore barbecue sauce—and if there is one, it certainly isn't this luxurious!) Also, don't miss the Sunday brunch, one of the most decadent in town.

JACOBSON

This is our best three-meal restaurant. It's reached by the only elevator in the city with a velvet-upholstered bench and the clientele is largely Asian, so the restaurant needs to satisfy their whims. That's why the kitchen has a top-notch sushi master, a dim-sum chef, and an Indian making the best tandoori in Las Vegas. The dining room is clean and sterile, the noise level subdued, the lighting bright. My favorite meal here is breakfast, not just because of the complimentary newspapers and filter coffee, but also for the rice porridge, a. k. a. congee. Lunch is a largely Asian affair, with pad Thai, great salt-and-pepper calamari, and an amazing lamb-shank curry leading the parade. Things are quieter during the evening, a good time to indulge in American cuisine, like 72-hour short ribs or halibut with green peppercorns. The twain have met.

CURTAS

The cool, sleek, somewhat boring design of the Mandarin Oriental's only three-meal-a-day restaurant lulls you into thinking you're in yet another all-things-to-all-travelers eatery. Think again, as Chef Shawn Armstrong and his team of international cooks turn out superior sushi, Thai specialties, top-flight tandooris, and even steak 'n' taters that admirably compete with restaurants specializing in such things. As befitting a Mandarin property, expect the Asian food to be exceptional (no matter what country you're eating that day), but the good old eggs Benedict (served over pulled pork) and banana-bread French toast might be even better than the (very good) dim sum. The whole point of the MOzen is to keep Arab potentates, Chinese high rollers, and Japanese moguls feeling as cosseted and well-fed as they do when they're exploiting the hoi polloi in their homelands, so be forewarned: The grub here is so good you'll feel like a Republican.

Author Picks

Royal tandoori platter; banana-walnut French toast;
congee; dim sum

The Rest of the Best

NOVE ITALIANO (West)

Italian

Palms
(702) 942-6800
n9negroup.com
Mon.-Thurs., 5:30-10 p.m.; Fri.-Sat., 5:30-11 p.m.; Sun., 1-7 p.m.
Expensive

JACOBSON

Chef Geno Bernardo is what the French call an auto-didact, meaning that he's self-taught. That at once frees a chef from rules he learns in cooking schools, or from mentors, enabling creativity. That may be the greatest strength of NOVE, which serves a killer Sunday brunch dubbed High Society and might have the most non-standard Italian menu in the city. Bernardo is a master of crudo, raw fish seasoned with olive oil, sea salt, and little else, a form that has become all the rage in our trendoid Italian restaurants. He's also a master of thin-crust pizza. His white-clam pizza, inspired by Frank Pepe's of New Haven, is probably the best pizza in Las Vegas. Bernardo's slow-simmered Sunday gravy is chockablock with almost disintegrated pork shoulder, as delicious as that of any Sicilian nonna. Combine all this with the ultra-hip fashion-model-gorgeous food servers, wine poured from inflatable kegs, and a matchless view of the Vegas valley and you have the best-kept secret among all our 50 Essential Vegas restaurants.

CURTAS

Las Vegas has two restaurants that defy the maxim that food gets worse the higher off the ground you go. This is one of them. It would be easy to dismiss NOVE as a playground for the sorts of playboys and playgirls who go to the Playboy Club one flight above, and it's true that more than a few celebrities of dubious taste make it to Geno Bernardo's Italian lair. But look past the hotties and the tatts and you'll find food that has few competitors. House-cured meats and vegetables grown in Geno's own Pahrump garden are featured, along with the requisite fresh pastas, a killer big-fish zuppa "guazzetto style," and a grilled whole branzino that tastes straight from the Amalfi Coast. Sunday afternoons are reserved for a boffo-enhanced buffet, featuring table dancing (as in: on top of the tables), loud music, and a plethora of drunken bimbos and himbos being gawked at by middle-aged food critics who should know better.

MANCINI

The first time I reviewed this place, I trashed it. Today, it's one of my favorite restaurants and Chef Geno Bernardo is one of my favorite chefs in town. He's a class act! While some assholes would respond with nasty letters and threats to my editor, he seemed determined to change my opinion. When I unsuccessfully tried to sneak unnoticed into NOVE's bar a few months after the review was published, he came out to greet me, informed me he'd changed many of the things I criticized, and sent out some dishes he thought I'd enjoy. His efforts have been so successful that I never even think of dining at NOVE's much hipper downstairs sister restaurant N9NE these days. The only place I eat in the Palms is NOVE. The steaks still don't wow me. (I prefer my beef dry-aged, which they don't offer.) But the Italian cooking is absolutely incredible. And Bernardo's grilled octopus is the best I've ever had.

Author Picks

Grilled octopus; cicchetti (small plates);
whole branzino; white-clam pizza

The Rest of the Best

OSTERIA DEL CIRCO [Strip]

Northern Italian

Bellagio
(702) 693-7223
bellagio.com
5:30-10:30 p.m., daily
Moderate

MANCINI

When Le Cirque patriarch Sirio Maccioni's three sons decided to strike out on their own, their goal was to get out of the suits and ties, as well as out from under the old-man's thumb—creating a more casual restaurant that could still live up to the family name. So they ditched the French cuisine and offered Italian dishes inspired by their mom's home cooking. But the famed Maccioni hospitality would never be compromised. The result was the original Osteria del Circo in New York. So when son Mario moved to Las Vegas to oversee our local incarnation of Le Cirque, he also opened a Sin City version of the brothers' pet project. Located directly next door to its formal French sister, Circo is a fun, whimsical, circus-themed room that offers jaw-dropping Italian cooking at more accessible prices. (Although it certainly isn't cheap!) And while ties are optional in most Las Vegas fine-dining restaurants these days (including Le Cirque), Circo has a more casual feel than most places with food this good.

CURTAS

Circo may not be the best Italian restaurant in town, but it is the most fun. Classics like Mama Egi's ravioli with butter and sage and the simple but stunning caccucio (fish stew) will always be on this menu, but Chef Massimilliano Campanari has injected new life into the kitchen with such dishes as branzino with braised fennel and grilled Napa quails

68

with Taggiasca olive tapenade. As with its sister restaurant Le Cirque next door, the service staff is relatively unchanged since the day the doors opened in October 1998 and even at its most crowded and hectic, there's an air of serene conviviality about this room. Patriarch Sirio is a frequent visitor to Las Vegas and at any given time, you might see him sitting in the corner, driving the managers crazy, but also ensuring that everyone here is treated like a VIP. Desserts by Philippe Angibeau are as mind-blowing and heart-stopping as you'd expect from a Maccioni restaurant.

JACOBSON

Circo has changed chefs several times during its run here, but one thing is always present: eminence grise Mario Maccioni, the scion of the Maccioni family, the man I like to call the accidental restaurateur. The gaudy Felliniesque atmosphere is still dazzling, as is the close-up view of the Bellagio fountains. Local power types still mourn the fact that the restaurant no longer opens for lunch and others criticize Sirio at Aria for being nothing more than a clone of the original, namely this joint. But for straight-up northern-Italian cooking, Circo still bats clean-up on any lineup card of our Italian restaurants. A fritto misto of shrimp, calamari, zucchini, and asparagus is unbeatable, as is the swordfish carpaccio, stirred-to-order risotti, and branzino alla griglia. This is the sort of place where the chefs whip up anything you want, from hand-made ravioli to the pasta sauce of your choice. And if you don't believe me, just ask Mario.

Author Picks

Tuscan soup alla Frantoiana; branzino; all pastas;
anything with pesto; all desserts

PAYARD PATISSERIE & BISTRO [Strip]   French

Caesars Palace
(702) 731-7110
caesarspalace.com
6-11 a.m., 11 a.m.-3 p.m., daily; Wed.-Sun., 5-10 p.m.
Moderate

JACOBSON

François Payard has literally jumped through hoops trying to make his poorly located Caesars Palace restaurant popular, and he finally seems to have done it. Foodies coast to coast mourned the passing of a menu filled with savories, such as his black-olive macaroon, but the concept proved to be too outré for the masses. Now that he's revamped dinner and serves a three-course lunch for $19.95 so tremendous even Curtas and Mancini agree that it's the best deal in town, the crowd is coming. This wedding-cake-like dining room, where Gregory Gourreau, a genius like his boss, plies his trade, is girlish and claustrophobic, but still worth an enthusiastic thumbs-up, since you get to watch the team do magic in a space no bigger than a studio-apartment kitchen. Payard's chocolates, pastries, and ice creams are more than just the best around; they could be the best in the country.

CURTAS

The best quiche in town, the best Croque Monsieur in town, the best eggs Benedict in town, and a chocolate-Nutella crêpe that will make you weep. That's our story and we're sticking to it. If this place were easier to find, it'd be three times the size and twice as expensive. As it is, uber-pastry chef François Payard's top toque in the kitchen, Gregory Gorreau, oversees a nonpareil pastry operation, as well as a cozy little 40-seat bistro and creperie tucked in off the beaten track inside Caesars. As good as the pastry, chocolates, and macaroons are, it's the savory dishes that set the standard for bistro cooking in Las Vegas. Since the recession, they've offered a three-course $19 lunch and dinner menu that may be the best deal in town. No matter what you order, the stunningly precise desserts will ensure you leave here on a sugar high note.

MANCINI

Because François Payard is best known as one of the world's great pastry chefs, most visitors to his restaurant stick to dessert or crêpes from the pastry side of the establishment. That's a shame, because Gregory Gorreau offers some of the most affordable French cuisine in town on his menus. The food is fairly simple, ranging from eggs Benedict and Croque Monsieur sandwiches to poussin (baby chicken) and Mediterranean sea bass. What makes it extraordinary is the perfectly executed French technique. And meals are served in one of the most playfully exotic dining rooms in the city—think Dr. Seuss on acid trying to design a wedding cake!

Author Picks

Mediterranean sea bass; mini-cheese soufflé; eggs Benedict; quiche; banana-Nutella crêpe

The Rest of the Best

PING PANG PONG (West)

Gold Coast
(702) 367-7111
goldcoastcasino.com
10 a.m.-3 p.m., 5 p.m.-3 a.m., daily
Inexpensive

MANCINI

The first time Max, John, and I sat down to discuss this book, it was at Ping Pang Pong's dim sum lunch. And while I've always liked dim sum, my knowledge of it pales in comparison to Max's. So eating the delicious dumplings with his guidance was one of the most educational culinary experiences I had in 2010. I've honestly never seen a better selection of dim sum in this town. And even if you aren't as familiar with them as Max and don't have an expert guide with you, they're rolled from table to table on a cart—allowing you either to point to whatever looks good or ask your server for guidance. The dinner menu also offers one of the most diverse selections of Chinese cuisine you're likely to find in a Vegas casino: squab and pork lettuce cups, steamed crab stuffed with sticky rice, a large selection of rice and noodle dishes, and seven varieties of the rice porridge congee.

CURTAS

The best dim sum in town, period. Unfortunately, you have to brave the environs of the Gold Coast to get to it. Go early, though, because by noon, any day of the week, the place is full of both Asians and Caucasians fighting for a table to get the good stuff. At night, this unassuming spot right off the casino floor finds lovers of authentic Cantonese cuisine rubbing elbows with nickel-slot junkies in their free T-shirts, who no doubt wonder what all the fuss is about. Those acquainted with delicacies like fish maw, abalone, and shark's fin can find them here, prepared every bit as finely as in the swankier hotels, but at relatively more reasonable prices. Anyone who orders sweet and sour pork ought to be shot—or at least forced to take a great leap forward to the nearest Panda Express. Service is multi-lingual, friendly, and efficient.

JACOBSON

I love owner Karrie Wu as much as her chicken feet, one of many dim sum served to a mostly authentic Chinese clientele inside the down-at-the-heels Gold Coast where she and her husband Kevin operate a noodle bar across the casino floor. This is the closest you'll come to Hong Kong in Vegas; servers speak marginal English, push rolling carts, and peddle savories and barbecued meat on platters. Kwei-lo, that's foreigner in the rough Cantonese dialect, love these sesame-studded shrimp rolls and chow fun fried rice noodles, but the Chinese prefer lo baak go, oily turnip cakes, cheung fan, a flat-rice-noodle wrap with barbecued pork, shrimp, or beef, and Chinese greens like ong choy, a reedy hollow green in the spinach family. One of my favorite dishes here is Night Market fried rice, a street dish laced with chili, beef, and tofu. To drink, there's bo lei cha, earthy Chinese red tea, a welcome respite from the insipid Jasmine variety most kwei-lo have forced on them.

Author Picks

Dim sum brunch; lo mai gai (sticky rice dumpling in lotus leaf)

The Rest of the Best

PRIME STEAKHOUSE (Strip)

Steakhouse

Bellagio
(702) 693-7223
bellagio.com
5-10 p.m., daily
Expensive

CURTAS

We're not saying Prime in Bellagio is expensive, but expect a dinner for four to run close to five Benjamins. No, we're not saying Prime is expensive, but our steaks were filets (excellent beef, small portions) and the Dover sole (the real enchilada: rich, buttery, flaky flesh, perfectly cooked) was also on the small side. Nah, we're not sayin' this place is expensive ... it's *real* expensive. Sean Griffin is at the helm, has some serious chops, and is in the kitchen every night—which is more than we can say for the guy whose name is on the door—Jean-George Vongerichten—who comes to Vegas about as often as I go to a monster-truck rally. But this place has bred some serious talent over the years—both mutton-chopped Wylie Dufresne and the languidly locked Kerry Simon used it as a jumping-off point—so feeding all those fat-cat carnivores must be good for career-launching. The décor, service, and wine program are all top drawer, but you'll pay through the nose for the privilege of basking in Vongerichten's absentee aura.

JACOBSON

Jean-Georges Vongerichten modernized his seminal Bellagio meat emporium, that of the grand drapes and Belle Epoque décor, down the street at Aria, and in many ways I prefer his new incarnation, with the egocentric eponymous Jean-Georges Steakhouse. Perhaps this globe-trotting chef still has an influence on Prime, but it's no more his steakhouse today than any other place on the Strip. All I can think of is the analogy that states that going to church on Sundays doesn't make you a Christian any more than being in a garage makes you a car. Still, this is the place for great steaks cooked in a vertical broiler at temperatures that would smelt pig iron and to partake of an insanely comprehensive wine list that has won a Wine Spectator Grand Award. This is also one of the best places in town to impress a client, date, or debtor. And if you ask nice, they might even let you out on the patio to eyeball the Bellagio Fountain show.

MANCINI

Las Vegas has more incredible steakhouses than you can shake a dead cow at. So for a place to stand out in my mind, it has to offer something very very special. What sets Prime apart for me is its elegance. Yes, I love the quality beef and I'm blown away by the house-made sauces and mustards that accompany it. But without the ambience, I probably wouldn't bother with the place. Prime is the only steakhouse in town to take a date for a really romantic dinner. Most of the other steakhouses seem like they were made for bachelor parties. Prime is where you go the night you want to propose to the girl of your dreams and where you'll want to return every year on your anniversary.

Author Picks

Rack of lamb with smoked-chili glaze and broccoli rabe; six peppercorn steak; soy rice-wine steak sauce

The Rest of the Best

RAKU (West)   Japanese

see map 1, page 147
5030 Spring Mtn. Rd. #2
(702) 367-3511
raku-grill.com
Mon.-Sat., 6 p.m.-3 a.m.
Moderate

CURTAS

Every chef and foodie in town makes a pilgrimage to the obscure corner of a rundown strip mall that houses this tiny 48-seat sanctuary of serious Japanese robatayaki cooking. In terms of finely tuned food, nothing off the Strip can match it. The menu is simplicity itself and your meal as small or large as you want to make it. Try the meat guts or bonito guts pickled in salt, or the tsukune (grilled ground chicken on a skewer), butter-sautéed scallop, bite-size foie gras bowl, pork ear, corn stuffed with potato, whole hokke fish (a Japanese mackerel), skewered tomatoes, and meltingly tender Kobe beef skewers that are so good you'll be speechless. Equally compelling are soy sauces and tofu made in-house, and a wine/sake/sochu list that's small, well-priced, and perfectly matched to the menu. Some say the Japanese put a finer point on their cuisine than anyone (even the French), and a tour around Chef Mitsuo Endo's cooking, with its small-plate perfection, will give you an idea what they're talking about.

JACOBSON

Endo expanded his postage-stamp-sized restaurant into a series of small labyrinthine rooms paneled in dark cherry and now it feels like the only real Japanese restaurant in Las Vegas. The chef's gastropub cooking is rarely encountered in this country: tofu with the texture of a silk-kimono sash; aju, Japanese river trout he has flown in fresh; and soboro gohan, minced chicken on top of steamed rice, garnished with briny pickles. There's a list of premium sakes available in flights of three or by the individual bottle. From dozens of char-grilled items cooked in the rear kitchen on an undersized hibachi, the most reliable choices include Kurobuta pork cheek, asparagus wrapped in bacon, or tsukune, fluffy ground chicken brushed with a soy glaze. If you insist, there are also fish guts, sea urchin, and pig's ear, all splendid with the large draughts of imported Japanese beer favored by the salary men at the tiny counter.

MANCINI

Everyone in town except Max refers to this tiny Japanese dining room as a robata restaurant. And while the phrase may not be technically correct (the food isn't served on paddles), this is the closest you'll find in Las Vegas to Tokyo's robatas, where small portions of various food are cooked over a charcoal grill. You'll also find hot and cold appetizers, rice and noodle dishes, and a selection of the Japanese stews known as oden. The selection is amazing. You can get everything from beef intestines and pigs ears to chicken thighs and vegetables. One thing you won't find is sushi, however, so don't bother asking. Nonetheless, the great selection of other dishes has made this one of the most popular places in town among restaurant-industry workers. It's open until 3 a.m. every night except Sunday, and after midnight you never know what celebrity chef you might spot grabbing an after-work snack here.

Author Picks

Poached egg with sea urchin and salmon roe; agedashi tofu

The Rest of the Best

RAO'S (Strip)

Caesars Palace
(877) 346-4642
caesarspalace.com
5-11 p.m., daily
Moderate

MANCINI

John and Max constantly question my love of the kind of down-home Italian food my grandmother used to make. And I'll admit I'm a sucker for simple pastas and sauces. But Rao's takes them to an undeniably world-class level. What blows my mind about this place isn't the complexity of the recipes. It's the fact that each is made to perfection every time I dine here. From the olive oil to the tomatoes, you can taste the quality of the ingredients from the very first bite. And Chef Carla Pellegrino's kitchen staff never seems to make an error in the cooking. Throw in her husband Frankie's charm and anyone who loves Italian cooking will pencil a visit to Rao's into every Vegas visit. If you can't make dinner here, drop by for lunch, the only time you can get Carla's delicious thin-crust pizzas. And ask host Bubbles (who looks like he came straight from a "Sopranos" casting call) about getting some time on the poolside bocce court.

CURTAS

Even if Carla Pellegrino wasn't a robo-babe, we'd still heart Rao's for bringing the best of red-sauce cuisine to a town that never met a bad Eye-talian joint it didn't love. Generic pasta and chicken parm fit Vegas like a fanny pack over a pair of 46-inch Sansabelts, but the Pellegrino gang has single-handedly changed that with superior meatballs, lemon chicken, fritto misto, linguine with clams, and veal smothered in hot and sweet cherry peppers that will have you singing "That's Amore." There's nothing complicated about this food, but it needs to be made with love and good ingredients, and that's just what Rao's does. It's virtually the same menu as the impossible-to-get-into New York original, which has made this out-of-the-way corner of Caesars a hit from the get-go, with celebs, goombas, and "Soprano"-channelers the world over. Dinner is always packed, but a relaxed lunch (with more than decent pizza) is served on the outdoor/indoor patio. Fuggeddabout wine and slug down a few highballs like Frank and Dino would.

JACOBSON

For decades, it was almost impossible to get a table at the East Harlem Rao's, which opened at the turn of the 20th century, so someone in the Pellegrino family, the current owners along with Ron Straci, got the bright idea to do one in Caesars Palace. It's still a tough table, but not an impossible one. Brazilian-born Italian-reared Carla Pellegrino cooks the family specialties with confidence: amazing meatballs, softballs of veal, beef, and pork, their most famous dish; lemon chicken, crisp, blackened, redolent of garlic, olive oil, and lemon juice; and my favorite dish here, clams Oreganate, seasoned stuffed clams served in their shells. This isn't innovative stuff, just the hearty peasant food of southern Italy where everyone eats family-style. The old joke about how to spot the Wasps at a Chinese restaurant (they're the ones not sharing the food) doesn't apply here. Don't even think about it. People have been whacked for less.

Author Picks

Linguine with shrimp and arugula; lemon chicken; pizzas

The Rest of the Best

ROSEMARY'S (West)

American

see map 2, page 148
8125 W. Sahara Avenue
(702) 869-2251
rosemarysrestaurant.com
Fri., 11:30 a.m.-2 p.m.; 5:30 p.m.-close, daily
Moderate

JACOBSON

Everyone who lives here knows how chef Michael Jordan and his wife Wendy defied the odds to establish the seminal neighborhood restaurant in Las Vegas, and everyone loves an underdog. Truth be known, I think Jordan has gotten better and better over the years, as he went from your basic Emeril Lagasse cut-out to an excellent chef in his own right. True, he no longer has his Mississippi-born wife helping him out in the kitchen, or her crazy mother Maggie, once a fixture in the dining room. And longtime manager Michael Shetler is now at Sage in Aria, so those frequent beer dinners are no more. But Jordan is still the best off-Strip chef in town and the restaurant has a loyal following. I like to come here for the best Bloody Mary in the world, the potato rolls, and the amazing barbecued shrimp—in short, Jordan's creative cooking. If you're wondering who Rosemary is, by the way, it's Jordan's mother. Mothers are big at Rosemary's.

Eating Las Vegas

CURTAS

June 19, 2010, marked the 11th anniversary of the opening of this stylish popular space on West Sahara. Can it be more than a decade since Michael and Wendy Jordan broke free of their Emeril bonds and struck out on their own? Does anyone remember that the odds of them succeeding were like 100 to 1 against? But survive they have, and Rosemary's remains one of our few upscale neighborhood success stories in the fine-dining department. Rosemary's food doesn't plow any new ground, the food isn't always as pristinely displayed as we might like, and sometimes we wish Jordan would back off on the number of ingredients he employs in a dish, but there's no denying his version of comfort food strikes the right note with his customers, who appreciate the quality, cooking, and ambience. I'd appreciate the place more if they took it easier with the starches and cream. But all wine is half-price on Sundays and superior cheeses and ales keep the bar busy, even if you're not in the mood for this or that atop creamed potatoes, grits, hoppin' john, or a risotto du jour.

MANCINI

The Jordans taught Las Vegas that fine dining doesn't have to be confined to the Strip. Hell, their attempt to open a second Rosemary's in the Rio proved to be a miserable failure. That's fine with the locals and tourists-in-the-know who pack the place nightly to enjoy creative yet approachable cooking, which is delivered at a price point well below what you'd pay for the same meal in a casino. This was also one of the first restaurants in town to offer microbrew pairings—a considerably more affordable option than the traditional wine pairings. True food geeks should make a reservation to dine at the "food bar" that overlooks the kitchen, where you can watch and chat with the line cooks up close and personal.

Author Picks

Pan-fried veal sweetbreads; shrimp with Maytag blue cheese and barbecue sauce; brick chicken; Maytag blue cheese soufflé

Aria at CityCenter
(877) 230-2742
arialasvegas.com
Mon.-Sat., 5-11 p.m.
Expensive

MANCINI

Aria has more world-class restaurants under one roof than most towns have within their city limits. Yet as much as I love so many of them, Sage is where I find myself returning time and time again. The massive, elegant '20s-style dining room, complete with gold-leaf wall, makes you feel as if you're expecting to be joined at any time by Jay and Daisy Gatsby. And the high-class speakeasy vibe of the lounge, which serves some incredible classic cocktails, completes the atmosphere. But the real reason to come here is to see how Chicago superstar Shawn McClain has succeeded in conquering Las Vegas. His contemporary fare is familiar, with some insane twists. The sublime foie gras custard brûlée is the most obvious, but don't visit without also trying his rich earthy take on yellowtail crudo or his Kusshi oysters with Tabasco sorbet and aged-tequila mignonette.

CURTAS

Shawn McClain made his mark in Chicago with Spring and Green Zebra, where he proved himself an innovative master of mixing culinary metaphors. Sage serves creative hyper-delicious food with a Midwestern sensibility that makes it all approachable for non-foodies as well as finicky gourmands. Resist the impulse to hang out at the bar over such gems as Vancouver Island Kusshi oysters dotted with a piquillo pepper/Tabasco sorbet, sharply seasoned Wagyu beef tartare, sinfully rich oxtail and beef-marrow crostini, sweet and sour sweetbreads, or foie gras custard brûlée, and make your way to the main dining room where these and other delights await in one of Vegas' most comfortable and dramatic spaces. The wine and craft-beer lists are full of well-priced lip-smacking surprises and the weekday happy-hour specials make this place a bargain-hunter's dream. Save room for dessert, as the pear tarte tatin with blue-cheese ice cream and canelés de Bordeaux are legendary.

JACOBSON

Shawn McClain impressed the living #$%A^ out of my colleagues, and indeed, Sage does have its moments. Sure, I like Kusshi oysters with a Bloody Mary sorbet, and most of his appetizers, especially an escargot and pork-belly agnolotti, and the innovative foie gras custard brûlée. I'd rather sit at the bar here, though, being sassed by Leann while she mixes my Aviation cocktail and nibble, than be stuck in the cavernous Art Deco dining room. I'd even praise the vegetarian entrées, such as slow-poached organic farm egg, which I'd definitely eat for breakfast. But the main dishes here aren't all that wonderful, save the Belgian ale-braised short ribs, and I think the boys have been overzealous in their enthusiasm. So while it's true that Sage deserves a place as one of the 50 Essentials, the cooking is spotty at times. The same cannot, however, be said of the excellent staff led by uber-GM Toby Peach. Service here rarely misses a beat.

Author Picks

Foie gras brûlée; sweetbreads; canelés de Bordeaux;
Kusshi oysters with Bloody Mary sorbet

The Rest of the Best

see map 2. page 148
8480 W. Desert Inn Road
(702) 871-7781
senofjapan.com
Mon.-Sat., 5 p.m.-2 a.m.; Sun., 5-mid.
Moderate

JACOBSON

I recently joked with the boys behind the counter at the superb Japanese ramen bar, Monta, that they
should rename the place the "Sick
of Taiwanese Sushi Noodle Bar."
What's wrong with sushi in Las Vegas? Not much, if you head to Sen,
where Japan-born Hiro Nakano, a
Nobu alum, treats his product with
the proper respect and the idiom of nigiri sushi with the correct un-
derstanding. And just what is sushi? Basically, it is short-grain Japanese
rice, cooked with a little vinegar and topped, stuffed, or wrapped with
fish, vegetables, or even fruit, emphatically not raw fish, which is called
sashimi in Japanese. In Japan, where nigiri, the form we favor, is a luxury, sushi is often made without fish, but rather toppings or stuffing with
egg, tofu, seaweed, or vegetables. The quality of the rice is the most
critical aspect of sushi and chef Nakano's is firm, fluffy, and flavorful, the
3 Fs. In fact, this is the best sushi in town, a literal temple to the stuff, if
it deserved one.

CURTAS

Japanese food is not about screaming orgasms and cream-cheese-
sushi concoctions (although Hiromi Nakano has some of them on his
menu to placate the Philistines). He respects his country's cuisine, his
ingredients, and his customers in dishing forth finely tuned food—at
prices that won't have you reaching for a respirator. The best way to
experience this is an omakase dinner (gently priced at either $55 or

$85 per) where his chefs compose a menu that builds through a ginger-spiced raw-seafood salad with mango, sparkling fresh kumamotos, and sablefish in that cliched miso glaze, to sushi that is as much about the sweetly scented perfect rice as it is about the perfect slices of fish lain about them. When they do accents to those fish, be it pickled eggplant or a spicy red-wine glaze, the flavors are accentuated just so, never by too much or too little, and every bite seems to be a revelation of the main ingredients—just the way Japanese food is supposed to be. His smoky, intense, miso soup is also the best we've tasted. The restraint and respect that Nakano and his chefs show for the underpinnings of their cuisine are rare among the Japanese restaurants of Las Vegas.

MANCINI

The appeal of this way-off-Strip Japanese restaurant can be summed up in five simple words: Nobu at half the price. Chef Hiro Nakano previously served as head chef at Nobu in the Hard Rock. Now he has his own westside restaurant where he offers the same type of delicious fusion cuisine and sushi. In fact, many would argue it's better than what's currently offered by his former employer. As with any great Japanese restaurant, the best way to dine here is to order one of the omakase tasting menus, in which the chef personally builds you a customizes a multi-course feast for you. But unlike most restaurants of this caliber, where omakase menus often start at over $100, Sen offers them for either $55 or $85 a person.

Author Picks

Ocean trout carpaccio; omakase dinner; sablefish with foie gras and wasabi aioli; tsukune (ground chicken on skewers)

The Rest of the Best

Bellagio
(702) 693-7223
bellagio.com
Mon.-Thurs., 5-9:45 p.m.; Fri.-Sun., 5-10:15 p.m.
Moderate

MANCINI

Chef Martin Heierling's beautiful dining room was overlooked for years, due to its location in a back corner of Bellagio. But all that's changed with the opening of CityCenter, as guests walking between the two resorts can't help but notice the place. The stone and flowing-water effects in the design give it the feel of a spa. But the real center-piece is the central glass-enclosed kitchen where the chefs work their magic. Separate teams cook in each quadrant, concentrating on one of the restaurants' several themes: seafood, grilled dishes, Asian cuisine, and Italian food. Rest assured, Heierling has worked all over the world and he and his staff are expert in all four.

CURTAS

Trying to be, by turns, a steakhouse, an Italian, an Asian, and an Indian eatery would seem to be a recipe for disaster. Somehow, though, Martin Heierling makes it work, dishing up serviceable standards of everything from potstickers and risotto Milanese to a meltingly tender signature short rib with horseradish mashed potatoes with real kick to them. As good as they are, it's the Indian tandoori selections that tend to tantalize us. The naan also seems a lot tastier here than in most of Vegas' mediocre Indian joints, ditto the superb savories from the tandoori grill and the raita and tamarind and mint sauces. So is Sensi really an Indian joint masquerading as an Italian steakhouse? Heierling would say not, but that's the way we prefer to think of it. Note: The house-made ginger ale is worth a trip all by itself, and this was one of the first bars in town to get on board the cocktail-nation train. It was KNPR's Cocktail Bar of the Year in '07. Desserts are a dream.

JACOBSON

I'm going to let you be content with what Al and John have to say about this place, other than putting in a plug for the ginger ale made by chef Heierling from a mysterious irresistible elixir, and talk more about Silk Road. Silk Road is Heierling's restaurant at the disastrous Vdara, still open for one of the best breakfasts in town, featuring a dish called Turkish eggs, and still open for lunch, although just barely. Silk Road is notable because it showcases Heierling's incredible creativity, which you get less of at Sensi for higher prices. Heierling cooks his Central Asian-inspired menu at Silk Road, oddball stuff you'll remember; kataifi-crusted shrimp and sardines with feta and mint come to mind. If you come to Sensi expecting this kind of creativity, though, you'll only get it from Japanese designer Super Potato's New Age design. Sensi is not what I'd call cutting edge, but the novelty of eating from four types of cuisines is still impressive, and the complimentary naan and chutney make it all worthwhile.

Author Picks

Tandoori surf & turf mixed grill; tandoori chicken; tom ka kai (shrimp soup); house-made ginger ale

The Rest of the Best

SETTEBELLO (South)

see map 3, page 149
140 S. Green Valley Parkway, Henderson
(702) 222-3556
settebello.net
11 a.m.-10 p.m., daily
Inexpensive

CURTAS

The best pizza in town, hands down. That pretty much says it all, but it doesn't explain why you should travel a dozen miles east of the Strip to the District at Green Valley Ranch for a taste of Neapolitan perfection. The crust is made with flour flown in from Italy, which gives it an unmatched puffy, soft, and chewy yeastiness. The toppings are all from top-shelf purveyors of cheese, vegetables, and various salumi. All pies are baked in a 900-degree wood-burning oven imported from Naples and the pizzaioli know their craft and churn out a pie about every 60 seconds. A fine selection of artisanal Italian beers helps wash all of this down and, while you're eating an out-of-this-world "Diavola" (with peppered salami), porchetta (with spicy roasted pork), or carbonara (with egg), you'll forget you're in the franchised-food capital of America.

JACOBSON

Brad Otton came to Vegas to be the strength coach at UNLV with his mentor, John Robinson. Then Robinson lost his job and Vegas gained a pizzeria. Otton, a personable former USC quarterback, learned pizza-making in Naples, where he was performing a two-year mission for the Latter-Day Saints church. He also learned Italian and became a fan of the Azzura, the Italian national soccer team. Otton is a devotee of the VPN, which translates as "real Neapolitan-style pizza." So expect a pie cooked in a wood-fired brick oven with a blackened bottom, the middle slightly soggy, and a crisp thin crust. To call this the best pizza in Las Vegas is an understatement. Otton himself makes terrific pizzas, but he has an ace-in-the-hole, an authentic pizzaiolo named Carmine, a native Neapolitan from Vico Equense, Italy, to fill in when he's not around. So his pizzas, topped with as little as possible, are almost always perfect.

MANCINI

To call Settebello family-friendly is the *biggest* understatement of this book. Just try finding a party eating here on a weekend afternoon without kids in tow (if you do, it'll probably be mine). And the staff is infinitely patient with the gaggles of rugrats who seem physiologically incapable of remaining in their seats—expertly dodging them with a smile as the younguns jump into and out of their chairs. The place is a godsend for parents with small children looking for a good restaurant where they won't be treated like lepers for bringing the whole family. Personally, however, I hate dining in places with a lot of kids acting like kids. So it's a testament to the quality of Settebello's thin-crust Neapolitan-style pizza that I'm willing to grin and bear them in order to enjoy this food of the gods. Perfect crusts, delicious sauce, and the highest-quality ingredients make this the finest pizza in town.

Author Picks

Quattro Stagioni pizza; carbonara pizza;
pizza Settebello; all pizzas; all Italian ales

The Rest of the Best

SIMON (West) American

Palms Place
(702) 944-3292
simonatpalmsplace.com
Sun.-Thurs., 7 a.m.-11 p.m.; Fri.-Sat., 7 a.m.-11:30 p.m.
Moderate

MANCINI

When it comes to all things Hollywood, there's a huge difference between being hip and trendy and being cool. It's the difference between *Twilight* and "Entourage," or between Paris Hilton and Johnny Depp. You either get that difference or you don't. Las Vegas has plenty of hip and trendy spots where beautiful people advertise their appearances, then sit in private booths and sip Cristal. Simon, on the other hand, is cool. Actors, rock stars, rappers, models, and adult-film actresses frequent this poolside restaurant simply to enjoy the atmosphere and the food. They love the casual relaxed vibe and the delicious familiar cuisine, which ranges from sushi and tandoori to the chef's famous meatloaf. And they love the admittedly overpriced Sunday brunch, where the wait staff and many guests arrive in their pajamas. Simply put, Simon is the coolest restaurant in town.

CURTAS

Kerry Simon used to be a serious chef. Now he runs a restaurant that specializes in not-so-serious food for the party-as-a-verb crowd. He made his Vegas rep on upscale bar food at the Hard Rock Hotel, then transferred that laid-back beautiful-people vibe to Palms Place, where flavor often takes a back seat to celebrity and eye-candy sustenance. Simon is probably as good as any three-meal-a-day restaurant in town, but the time to go is for the Sunday "pajama" brunch, where hungover hipsters come to the see and be scene. If food is a priority, stick with the pizzas, crispy rock shrimp, simple salads, and steaks, and avoid the sushi. Al Mancini loves this place; he thinks its mega-cool and it is. But I'm not sure he's ever actually paid attention to the food, and I'm not sure Simon actually does either.

JACOBSON

In a perfect world, Kerry Simon would have been in the E Street Band, playing rhythm guitar. We won't tell you how old he is, but it's more or less a given that he remembers Paul McCartney before he was a Wing and anyone who knows him will attest to that. I think of him as a sort of chef's Jack LaLanne. You probably won't catch him eating the kind of comfort foods that made him famous: chicken and waffles, the best meatloaf in Las Vegas, chicken curry, or mock Hostess snowballs. My last meal at Simon was a doozy; the killer Sunday brunch with that do-it-yourself Bloody Mary bar. Simon, meanwhile, if he's seen at all, will be sipping a celery and beet milkshake, not dunking shrimp in his peerless Remoulade sauce or nibbling on his famous caramel corn. Or he might be eating some of the sushi his sushi master prepares for the brunch, but that would be pushing it for him.

Author Picks

Tuna dynamite; banana-leaf halibut; popcorn shrimp

SOCIETY CAFE (Strip)

Continental

Encore
(702) 248-3463
encorelasvegas.com
Sun.-Thurs., 7 a.m.-11 p.m.; Fri.-Sat., 7-1 a.m.;
Late Night Menu, 11 p.m.-3 a.m.
Moderate

MANCINI

Calling Society a "coffee shop" is a little like calling a Ferrari a "car," calling the *Queen Mary 2* a "boat," or calling Megan Fox an "attractive young woman." This restaurant brings the concept of a casino coffee shop to a level never before seen in Las Vegas. The bright Oscar Wilde-inspired décor is simultaneously fun and elegant—and the same goes for the food. The breakfast menu alone rocks my world! (And this is coming from someone who rarely rolls out of bed before noon.) Frosted Flake French toast with caramelized bananas and chocolate cream and pumpkin and buckwheat pancakes with pumpkin butter and candied pecans are tempting. But I can never seem to resist the steak-and-egg sliders: a "grown-up" take on an Egg McMuffin made with filet mignon, scrambled eggs, and creamed spinach on a bacon-cheddar muffin. The lunch and dinner menus offer similarly tempting treats.

CURTAS

Chef Kim Canteenwalla (and his wife Elizabeth Blau) serve up a coffee shop that is by turns lovely to look at and pleasing to taste at prices that won't choke you—at least at lunch. Dinner for two can easily exceed $150 if you go hog wild, much less if you stick with small plates. Canteenwalla and crew have made gourmet upscale bar food a specialty, with basics like burgers, wings, dips, and nibbles done to the nth degree. Nothing will scare or intimidate Grandma (or a nine-year-old, for that matter), but everything seems to be one of the best versions of comfort food you've ever come across. There are staples like superb steak salad, pea soup, mac 'n' cheese, pretzel bread, a ham-and-cheese sandwich, and mini-quiches done at a very high level—and consumed in a grand-salon setting that could be straight from La Belle Epoque. They won't make you cancel your reservation at Alex, but do go down quite nicely with one of Patricia Richard's specialty cocktails.

JACOBSON

If any great Vegas cook flies under the radar, it's the unassuming Canadian Chef Kim Canteenwalla. He's done work in Singapore, at the MGM Grand as Executive Chef, and in many exotic ports of call, so the eclectic menu at Society won't come as a big surprise. This emporium of kid-food fare serves things like chicken lollipops, pigs in a blanket, and Whoopie pie. Steve Wynn, amazingly, is now a vegan, and in his image, the menu has sprouted fare like purée of corn soup and vegetable flatbread with artichoke, eggplant, vegan cheese, and roasted peppers. I usually come here for the Frosted Flake French toast with maple syrup at breakfast, but the chef's amazing chopped salad made with organic turkey, his Philadelphia cheesesteak-stuffed potstickers, and an incredible Jidori chicken tasting reel me in often. There will probably be a dozen new creations here by the time you read this.

Author Picks

Steak and egg sliders; buffalo wings;
beans 'n' franks; pork-belly potstickers

SPAGO [Strip]

Forum Shops, Caesars Palace
(702) 369-6300
wolfgangpuck.com
Café: Sun.-Thurs., 11:30 a.m.-11 p.m.,
Fri.-Sat., 11:30 a.m.-midnight
Dining Room: 5:30-10 p.m., daily
Moderate

CURTAS

The granddaddy of all famous Vegas eateries (opened December 13, 1992) and still performs at an exceptionally high level, thanks to the ministrations of the Puck fine-dining empire and Chef Eric Klein. Klein was a seasonal locavor-driven chef years before food magazines were paying attention and his Alsatian/California/French-flecked food reflects his obsessions. In wintertime, we come for the choucroute (off the menu). But the rest of the year, just about anything from the pizzas and pastas to Wolfgang's famous Wienerschnitzel is always top drawer. Locals Food Alert: Even at the busiest times, Spago holds back a table or two for locals. Announce that you're from Las Vegas and you're likely to be seated quicker than others without a reservation. Fun Fact Number Two: The Wolf Gang are big supporters of the Las Vegas art scene and the works of local artists are featured in the restaurant, most prominently the giant Tim Bavington hanging on the big wall. Fun Fact Number Three: The people-watching from the café is some of the best in town.

MANCINI

Spago has held a special place in my heart ever since the gorgeous and fabulous Gena Gershon flirtatiously toyed with the naïve Elizabeth Berkley on its Forum Shops patio in the film *Showgirls*. You may never come across a lunch meeting quite that sexy here, but this is still the power-lunch spot in town. The deals made in Spago have shaped Las Vegas for nearly two decades. And of all Puck's Vegas restaurants, none captures the chef's eclectic creative personality better than this one. You'll find sashimi, quesadillas, pastas, steaks, and Asian dishes. And the lunch menu offers a selection of the pizzas that made Wolfgang Puck a household name, including the smoked-salmon version. Eric Klein selects his products under his mentor's strict guidelines to make sure animals are sustainable and raised in cruelty-free conditions. And he's more than happy to indulge vegetarians or vegans. (If you want a veggie meal, it's better to call a day or two early, but the chef can also accommodate such requests on short notice.)

JACOBSON

P-man has Eric Klein in the kitchen, so he can rest easy. (And that goes for you too, Robins.) Klein's amazing choucroute garnished with homemade sausages, the seminal smoked-salmon pizza Robin Leach claims to have invented, the big eye tuna, and Kenny Magana's cookie plate are all the stuff dreams are made of. So now it can be said: Wolf, Arnold's English is better. Perhaps you're aware the Governator went belly up in a restaurant of his own called Schatzi. I can't say what kind of a governor Wolf would be, but California Cuisine owes a debt to Arnold's fellow Austrian. At a teenager, Wolf hid in a potato cellar to escape apprenticeship, but he stuck it out. When he opened Spago Las Vegas, he stood at the entrance with his then-GM, Gerard Izard, looked at his empty room, and said he had made a mistake. History has proven him wrong. To paraphrase what Cagney said in *Yankee Doodle Dandy*, "The Strip thanks you, the tourists thank you, and I thank you."

Author Picks

Pan-seared breast of duck; smoked-salmon pizza; choucroute garni; Alsatian tarte flambée

THE STEAK HOUSE [Strip]

Steak and Seafood

Circus Circus
(702) 734-0410
circuscircus.com
Sun.-Fri., 5-10 p.m.; Sat., 5-11 p.m.
Moderate

MANCINI

Whenever a large group of male friends comes to town (usually for a bachelor party), the first thing they ask me is where they can find a good old-Vegas-style steakhouse. And they're always surprised when I recommend THE Steak House at Circus Circus. Sure, the hotel's a dump. It's always packed with kids. (More accurately, it's always packed with young couples who look barely past puberty, but somehow seem to have a litter of kids in tow.) So, if you don't have toddlers of your own, there are only two reasons to set foot in the place. The first is to relive Hunter S. Thompson's famed ether trip at the Horse-A-Round Bar. And the second is to visit the steakhouse, a tiny enclave of civilization tucked away in a corner of the casino. Beef is dry-aged behind glass walls and the dimly lit booths are reminiscent of the Rat Pack days. And the already-low steak prices include vegetables, soup or salad, and a side dish.

CURTAS

The billboard on I-15 proclaims it: "BRANDED THE BEST (STEAK-HOUSE) FOR 20 YEARS IN A ROW." It's not. It's not even in the top 10. But it does deliver the best bang for the buck in aged steer muscle in town. First though, you have to brave the shopworn smelly environs of Circus Circus. The restaurant—warm, clubby, and man-musty—is accessible by a short walk from the back parking lot, bobbing and weaving among the shoddiest bunch of turistas in Vegas. Try not to get depressed with what you witness, for once inside you'll find a pretty decent Caesar salad, a 21-day dry-aged strip, some good pretzel bread, and a pedestrian Key lime pie. And the $42 porterhouse is probably the best deal in town. No one's ever going to mistake this place for CUT, Craftsteak, or Carnevino, but for what it is—an old-fashioned place to get some steak 'n spuds—you could do a lot worse. And its competition could learn a thing or two from its small, but well-priced, wine list. Speaking of wine, it also has a very relaxed corkage policy.

JACOBSON

I was too lazy to veto this place, or maybe I left it in because I know your Uncle Tony is going to insist on eating here. But let's face it. Las Vegas Boulevard is lined with excellent steakhouses, stretching clear down to the underrated Twin Creeks at the Silverton where the food is a damned sight better than it is at this old warhorse. I'm a fan of the Old Vegas décor and the price point here does beat most of the competition. Another plus is a mesquite broiler, if you like the taste of the mesquite (I do) and don't mind that it tends to dry meat out (I don't). Still, if you were asked to write down this menu without looking at it, you'd get an A-. I prefer creativity in a steakhouse, but if you insist, start with black-bean soup or grilled garlic shrimp, order any of the 21-day aged Prime steaks with confidence, and ask yourself why you aren't eating down the street at CUT or Prime.

Author Picks

Bone-in ribeye; New York strip; baked potato; Caesar salad

The Rest of the Best

TODD'S UNIQUE DINING (South)   Contemporary

see map 3, page 149
4350 E. Sunset Rd., Henderson
(702) 259-8633
toddsunique.com
Mon.-Sat., 4:30-10 p.m.
Moderate

MANCINI

When it comes to upscale off-Strip dining, the west side has Rosemary's and the east side has Todd's. This place is the best restaurant you'll find on this side of Las Vegas Boulevard. Tucked into an unassuming strip mall, the dining room is comfortable enough to stop by for happy-hour snacks at the bar, but fancy enough to visit on a special night out. The menu similarly walks the line between neighborhood restaurant and fine dining. Entrées include seared ahi tuna with wasabi mashed potatoes and soy garlic sauce, meatloaf with caramelized-onion mashed potatoes and mushroom cabernet sauce, and sea scallops with wild-mushroom potatoes and pistachio butter. Everything is prepared by chef and owner Todd Clore, who put in his time on the Strip at Bally's Sterling Brunch before deciding to bring his exceptional cooking to Green Valley. And while Todd runs the kitchen, his wife Terry minds the front of the house, making sure every guest is treated like family.

CURTAS

You can count on one hand the number of locally owned chef-driven restaurants worth traveling to. Todd Clore's small and very personal restaurant, located in the heart of Green Valley, has been wooing customers since 2004 with its Cal-Ital-French-Mediterranean-influenced cuisine that's far more sophisticated than you'd expect this many miles from the Strip. Clore's wine dinners are legendary (and sell out quickly) and, like the food, are priced to please. Much of the menu is set in stone (his goat-cheese wontons, halibut teriyaki, and braised short ribs are justifiably famous), but Clore tweaks it every so often to keep the fussy foodies happy. Because it's the only gourmet game in town—in the restaurant-starved environs of Monochrome (a. k. a. Green) Valley—Todd's has the feel of a neighborhood hangout. After one meal here, though, you'll feel like one of the gang.

JACOBSON

All the good Vegas restos are on the Strip. Well, personable Todd Clore has something to say about that. Yes, his restaurant is modest, the booths are uncomfortable, and the location, a non-descript mall hard by a Joe's Crab Shack, is as suburban as a Desperate Housewife. But his eclectic resumé, including a stint in an Orange County Chinese restaurant and as a buffet chef on the Strip at Bally's, serves him well, as does his solid technique and the way he sources quality products not necessarily reflected in the prices. It all adds up to a restaurant you'll want to return to again and again. Asian potstickers with a piquant dipping sauce, delicious tuna tartare on crispy rice cakes, steak "on fire" sluiced with black beans, and Lake Superior whitefish are just a few of Clore's better creations. A meal on the Strip at this level will cost twice as much.

Author Picks

Goat-cheese wontons; skirt steak on fire

The Rest of the Best

TOM COLICCHIO'S CRAFTSTEAK [Strip]   Steakhouse

MGM Grand
(702) 891-7318
mgmgrand.com
Sun.-Thurs., 5:30-10 p.m.; Fri.-Sat., 5:30-10:30 p.m.
Expensive

JACOBSON

OK, I admit it. I haven't eaten at Craftsteak for more than two years. During that time, Tom Colicchio established himself as a national celeb and a TV fascist, sending young dewy-eyed hopeful chefs to doom on his TV show "Top Chef" and reducing the egos of famous chefs such as Rick Moonen to rubble on "Top Chef Masters" (where Moonen was given the heave-ho by legendary crybaby prima donna Markus Samuelsson). His MGM restaurant hasn't suffered, thankfully. It's still the best place in Vegas for a healthy piece of grass-fed beef and one of the only places in town to eat delicacies such as hen-of-the-woods mushrooms and other exotic produce Colicchio keeps on his menu. The bar has a legendary list of fine spirits, especially Scotch and Cognac, and the dining room boasts one of the most modern and urban feels in Las Vegas. Craftsteak has had many chef changes over the years, but the food never changes. The boss is such an *éminence grise*, his presence is never far away, despite the fact that he's almost certainly on a golf course or around a TV studio, not in an actual kitchen.

CURTAS

It used to be just "Craftsteak," but given the popularity of "Top Chef," combined with the more aggressive marketing brought on by the Great Recession, it's now Tom Colicchio's Craftsteak. For most restaurants, the recession has meant cutbacks, reductions, and enticing customers with the occasional bargain or early-bird special. For Craftsteak—or, excuse me: Tom Colicchio's Craftsteak—his celebrity means you'll pay dearly for the privilege of basking in his (absentee) aura. By dearly, we mean: $64 for an eight-ounce Wagyu flat-iron steak or $36 for a 12-ounce hangar. Mere mortals shouldn't even think of eating a premium cut. Slightly more affordable are the beautiful heirloom vegetables, fungi, and tubers that comprise the right side of the menu. Tokyo turnips, anyone? Most of these veggies are so good you'll be tempted to compose a meal without any protein in it and you'd be making the right decision. The wine list is broad, thick, and deep, but no one without a trust fund can afford the bottles. In a town full of ridiculously priced lists, this one may be the worst.

MANCINI

Forget about John's whining about the prices of his precious vino! Drinking wine here is for wimps and old ladies! Cut to page 69 of the 100-page wine list and order yourself a real man's drink! What sets Craftsteak apart from the billion other great steakhouses in town—other than the celebrity chef with his name on the door—is the spirits program. We're talking 18 pages of Scotch and more than 20 bourbons. If you feel a little overwhelmed, the sommelier has put together 10 different Scotch flights, each of which offers three-quarters-of-an-ounce pours of three varieties, side by side, for anywhere from $17 to $1,215.

Author Picks

Flight of fine Scotch; Wagyu hangar steak; grass-fed beef; anything but the overpriced wine

The Rest of the Best

TOP OF THE WORLD RESTAURANT [Strip]   American

Stratosphere
(702) 380-7711
stratospherehotel.com
11 a.m.-3 p.m., daily
Sun.-Thurs., 5:30-10:30 p.m.;
Fri.-Sat., 5:30-11 p.m.
Expensive

CURTAS

The farther you get off the ground, the old saying goes, the worse the food gets, with airplanes being the prime example. Under the recent guidance of two experienced chefs, Claude Gaty and Rick Giffen, the menu here teems with French-Asian flavors and might single-handedly put that old axiom out to pasture. About the only thing not to like about TOTW is the logistical problem it has always had: Getting to it is a bitch. But it's worth the trek, because once you arrive, you'll be seated in one of the most spectacular restaurant settings in the world. They could probably serve warmed-over tacos here and be successful, but the upscale dining room takes its food seriously, with such highlights as Yucatan shrimp ceviche, jumbo prawns a la plancha, and a horseradish-crusted prime rib that's a thing of beauty. Sommelier Dean Wachsletter has been here since the opening (1996) and his well-chosen wine list has remarkably down-to-earth prices for being served from such a lofty perch.

JACOBSON

Top of the World doesn't have to be good to stay busy. Like several of the restaurants on Fisherman's Wharf in San Francisco, they could put oatmeal on the menu and still fill the room. The kicker is that Goldman Sachs, the giant investment firm blamed for everything from our bad economy to the chickenpox, is the new owner. The group has gone the extra mile, hiring seasoned chefs Claude Gaty and Rick Giffen. I could care less the restaurant takes 80 minutes to do a full revolution. When I look down on Las Vegas as we spin slowly, I feel like James Stewart in the film *Vertigo*. I'm certifiably insane for Giffen's deconstructed shrimp cocktail, though, and Gaty's tater tots with foie gras, a dish tastier than Montreal's famous foie gras-topped poutine, is, as French say, "vaut le voyage." I am piqued at the idea of having to pass through a security checkpoint to take a long elevator ride, but what the hell.

MANCINI

For years, Top of the World's reputation was simple: The view was spectacular, but the overpriced mediocre food was enough to make you want to plunge off the Stratosphere's observation deck. Claude Gaty and Rick Giffen, who took over the kitchen in 2010, have changed all that. The food is now at least equal to the panoramic view from your table, which rotates once per hour to let you take in the entire valley over the course of your meal. But don't be surprised if jumpers still interrupt your meal. The newest Stratosphere thrill ride allows tourists to harness themselves to a safety line on the top of the tower and plunge 830 feet to a second-story roof—falling directly past the windows of the restaurant. Those occasional distractions notwithstanding, Top of the World now truly deserves its reputation as one of the most romantic restaurants in town.

Author Picks

Miso black cod with ponzu butter sauce; tater tots with foie gras; horseradish-crusted prime rib; Kurobuta pork chop

VALENTINO (Strip)

Italian

Venetian
(702) 414-3000
valentinorestaurantgroup.com
5:30-10:30 p.m., daily; Grill 11:30 a.m.-3:30 p.m., 4:30-10:30 p.m., daily
Moderate

JACOBSON

Piero Selvaggio was reluctant to open a branch of his Santa Monica Italian restaurant here, but his good friend Wolfgang Puck encouraged him and the Venetian's curmudgeonly owner Sheldon Adelson had the good sense to make him an offer he couldn't refuse. (Selvaggio is the Sicilian here, not Adelson, just to keep the record straight.) Then Piero had the good sense to send his best employee, Luciano Pellegrini, to Vegas as chef/partner. That's the main reason the restaurant has thrived for more than a decade. Looch, as he's known by most of us, is as solid a performer as there is. It doesn't hurt that the restaurant has the best Italian wine list in the city and Piero's presence, when he's in town, is a huge plus. (He's the most charming host anywhere.) It's a shame the hotel has co-opted Selvaggio by putting more Italian joints on property than there are in Hoboken, New Jersey. Still, Valentino is a top performer and the up-to-date northern Italian fare can't be beat.

CURTAS

Valentino in Santa Monica has been known as one of the best Italian restaurants in the country for more than 30 years. Our Valentino has only been here for nine, but it remains at the top of our pasta list (only B&B is in the same league) and is probably the best under-the-radar place in town. The wine bar and café out front are in many ways preferable to the dark cave-like main restaurant, but regardless, what Luciano Pelligrini and his crew do with noodles, game, beef, and small birds is nothing short of amazing. Even if you don't have time for a full meal, stop by the wine bar, tuck into a plate of hickory-smoked quails with a fig-vincotto dressing, sip a nice Zenato Ripassa Valpolicella, and you'll see why Italian food and wine lovers flock here.

MANCINI

Sure, Piero Selvaggio is the guy with his name on the door. But in Las Vegas, Lucciano Pelligrini is nearly as big a celebrity as his boss. This restaurant takes Italian cuisine to a gourmet level that would make most French chefs jealous, yet is just as comfortable honoring its rustic roots. One minute he's delicately balancing perfectly prepared quail, foie gras, and fava beans, and the next he's knocking your socks off with a deceptively simple wild-boar ragout. And one of his coolest touches is a tasting menu taken directly from Sevlaggio's cookbook that even provides the page number of each dish served. (So at least we can dream of matching Pelligrini's genius.) I'm not a huge fan of the décor, but the private Barolo Room, which can actually seat up to four, may be the most romantic spot in town for a two-person meal.

Author Picks

Pasta with wild-boar ragout (in season);
white-truffle risotto (in season); mascarpone-stuffed bucatini;
risotto with field greens and pecorino

The Rest of the Best

VINTNER GRILL (West)   American

see map 2, page 148
10100 W. Charleston Blvd.
(702) 214-5590
vglasvegas.com
Mon.-Fri., 11 a.m.-10 p.m.; Sat., 4-11 p.m.; Sun., 4-10 p.m.
Moderate

JACOBSON

Vintner Grill might be my favorite success story among all of our restaurants. The spiffy décor, including a black-and-white-checked floor and elegant patio cabanas, would be enough to bring in most of us, even without Matthew Silverman's colorful intelligent cooking. But the restaurant has connected successfully with the Summerlin crowd and has become a de facto social club as well. Part of the credit goes to the terrific bar scene here and Sommelier Troy Kumalaa's excellent wine list, which features, among other things, 50 bottles for less than fifty dollars each. From a menu that changes daily, don't miss the good wood-fired flatbreads or pasta with lamb Bolognese for lunch, or Prime meats from the wood-fired grill at supper, such as the marinated skirt steak with whole-grain mustard. The only problem with the place, in fact, is finding it. You might drive by three or four times before you'll figure out where it's hidden.

MANCINI

Another one of Las Vegas' great neighborhood restaurants, it's the nature of this particular neighborhood that gives Vintner its unique character. Located in the wealthy suburb of Summerlin, the crowd here feels a bit more formal and uptight than those at Todd's and Rosemary's—as does the menu. But the food is just as well-prepared and the pastas are particularly amazing. Throw in the stunning modern white décor and Vintner delivers a unique dining experience that lies somewhere between that of a Strip power spot and a neighborhood restaurant. The only things that seem out of place here (other than my punk-rock ass) are the video poker machines at the bar. But owner Michael Corrigan's first restaurants were the much more casual RoadRunner chain and he apparently can't get away from the instinct to rely on gaming to help pay a place's rent.

CURTAS

It's easy to dismiss VG as a hangout for the rich white people who call Summerlin home, but if you look closely, you see a serious gastronomic restaurant that's a lot better than it has to be. Matthew Silverman plays his menu off an ambitious wine program and it's hard not to be impressed by his superior fried calamari, original pastas (tagliatelle with lamb Bolognese, crab ravioli with English peas, et al.), and a bouillabaisse that's astonishingly good for being 250 miles from the nearest ocean. Power lunchers invade daily, and those looking for something tastier at night will find the bar stocked with lots of unique beers and ales, as well as plenty of cougars and clock-ticking 30-somethings out to meet their next nouveau-riche ex-husband.

Author Picks

Pan-seared diver scallops with sweet-corn risotto;
pasta with lamb Bolognese; Vosges chocolate tasting

The Rest of the Best

YELLOWTAIL [Strip]

Sushi

Bellagio
(702) 693-7223
bellagio.com
Mon.-Thurs., 5-10 p.m.; Fri.-Sun., 5-11 p.m.
Moderate

MANCINI

Nightclub kings The Light Group operate a total of six restaurants in Las Vegas: Fix, Stack, Union, Brand, Diablo's Cantina, and Yellowtail. And since most are located close to one of the organization's clubs, they're always packed with beautiful celebrities looking for a late-night snack before they pose for the paparazzi on a red carpet. Despite that, I still like all of those places. But Yellowtail makes this list because it's several steps above its sister restaurants. This isn't just a fun, trendy, pre-party spot. It's a serious destination in its own right. Pro-snowboarder-turned-chef Akira Back is at his best when creating innovative raw-seafood dishes (calling them sushi doesn't do the food justice). Standouts include lobster carpaccio with sweet shaved onion, cilantro, and ponzu, and his Thai snapper with olive oil, shiso, and tosazu. And celebrity-spotters will still get a chance to see some stars here. Taylor Swift once Tweeted she had "the best meal of my life" at Yellowtail.

CURTAS

Yellowtail shines with its sushi, even though it has no sushi "bar." Everything is ordered off-menu and composed out of sight, but the fish is artfully sliced, the right size, firm to the bite, and not burdened by anyone's attempt to jazz it up. A plate of signature sushi items holds delicate lightly seared toro of good quality, kimedai (Japanese Golden Eye snapper), braided kohada (barely marinated sardines that don't taste like cheap pickled herring), firm and chewy mizukado (octopus), and a Santa Barbara prawn that tastes like it was caught that morning. The rice is delicate, the right size, shaped well, slightly warm, and full of infused flavor. None of these competes with a top-of-the-line sushi boutique on either coast, but for a volume restaurant in a large hotel, you'd be hard-pressed to find better seafood or presentation. Horn dogs take note: There's so much cleavage hanging around the bar here some nights you half expect them to start lactating into your cocktails.

JACOBSON

Yellowtail, not the cheap wine from Australia, but a Japanese fusion space in Bellagio specializing in hand rolls, sushi, and sashimi, could be one of dozens of places cloned throughout the big American cities. But that's OK, because the concept has legs. The Light Group tends to make its spaces agreeable to Gen X and Gen Y'ers, and that's exactly what they did here when they changed the stodgier Shintaro over to this concept. Former snowboarder Akira Back is both Korean and Japanese and his dishes reflect his dual background. The sake list is formidable, and such dishes as signature yellowtail tartare with wasabi-flavored soy sauce, big-eye tuna pizza, and Maine-lobster carpaccio make the libations go down easy. The striking design is by David Rockwell, and he's made the space hip and cheerful. But the top tables in here are still the ones facing the Bellagio Fountains, as they were when the restaurant was its former incarnation.

Author Picks

Lobster carpaccio; uni; Scottish salmon on rice cracker with Japanese hollandaise; yari ika (needle squid); big-eye tuna pizza

The Rest of the Best

Golden Caviar at Sensi, Bellagio

Section III

Vetoes,
Additional Recommendations,
and More

Margherita Pizza at Wolfgang Puck Bar & Grill, MGM Grand

Vetoes

The arguments over which restaurants to include in this book were spirited, heated, and frequently ugly. But our rule from the beginning was that all three authors had to unanimously support a restaurant's inclusion on this list. So after the fights, debates, logical arguments, and personal attacks, one side usually conceded. Occasionally, the opponent of a restaurant was swayed to see the merits of its inclusion on what we all consider an extremely prestigious list. More frequently, a restaurant's champion realized that he couldn't win, then threw up his hands and grudgingly accepted defeat.

But there were a handful of times when the fight didn't end.

The restaurants that follow are the places that didn't make the list, despite the fact that at least one of us felt they *absolutely needed* to be included in this book in order for us to retain our credibility. In each case, the nominating party felt his choice represented part of the heart and soul of the Las Vegas restaurant scene. And in each case, one of his co-authors told him there was no way in hell he'd put his name on a list that included that restaurant. As you'll read, our reasons for vetoing a restaurant ranged from personal gripes about an experience in a place to grand philosophical stands about the nature of a particular type of restaurant. And sometimes one of us just thought the other was a complete idiot for liking a place that sucks. In the end, the reason didn't matter. Without unanimous consent, a restaurant simply couldn't make the Essential 50.

Many restaurateurs will undoubtedly label us assholes for not including their establishment in this book. That's fine—we've each been called "asshole" so many times that we've come to wear it as a badge of honor. But we're not cowards! So for these hardest-fought vetoes, we're stepping up and putting our names on them.

What follows is a much more civilized version of the arguments that went on while writing this book. We've only included the restaurant's most vocal supporter and its most vocal critic, since the third vote really didn't matter.

CAFE MARTORANO   Italian

Rio
(702) 221-8279
cafemartorano.com
6 p.m.-10:30 p.m., daily

NOMINATED BY JACOBSON

Yes, it can be loud in here, although muscleman Steve Martorano was responsive enough to turn down the deafening noise level of the music videos after enough people complained. But I love these meatballs and pork feet, and many other dishes can be sheer poetry. Mancini thinks I don't like goomba food, as he calls it, but he's wrong. Café Martorano makes a melt-in-the-mouth marinara, an amazing eggplant stack, and a number of pastas I can't stop eating. I'd come back just for a meatball, made with veal, pork, and beef, plus a few bread crumbs and more than a little Parmesan cheese. Portions are so huge, I usually eat the leftovers for days. I've said it before and I say it again. Martorano is the Godfather of Vegas Italian cooking.

VETOED BY CURTAS

Italian-Americans spent 50 years trying to overcome the low-rent goomba image 1950s' America foisted upon them—and that many current goombas now take to like a secretary to a spray tan. "Mr. Irresistible" Steve Martorano asks them (and us) to embrace his wife beaters, his too many tatts, and his lotsa pasta and meatball menu because of those signifiers and the current douchebag trend they trade upon. The thought of making his food embraceable to anyone but a bunch of meatballs has apparently never occurred to him. This place also fancies

Eating Las Vegas

itself as a restaurant-cum-nightclub and Stevie insists you listen (and we mean *listen*) to his non-stop favorite tunes throughout your meal of mediocre chicken, veal, and macaroni dishes. "Soprano" wannabes and "Jersey Shore" aficionados will love it. Anyone with any taste won't.

FIREFLY   Tapas

3900 Paradise Road
(702) 369-3971
fireflylv.com
11:30 a.m.–2 a.m., daily
Plaza Casino
(702) 380-1352
Sun.–Thurs., 5–10:30 p.m., Fri.–Sat., 5 p.m.–midnight

NOMINATED BY MANCINI

The original Firefly location on Paradise Road has long been a Las Vegas institution. The crowd is generally young and artsy, the tapas are tasty and reasonably priced, the sangria is strong, and the outdoor patio is great when the weather is right. Firefly's second location shares much of the same menu, but is located in the second-story saucer of the admittedly past-its-prime Plaza Hotel and Casino downtown. The room (featured in the film *Casino* when it was a fine-dining restaurant) offers the best view in town of the Fremont Street Experience. And the place has become the most popular downtown dining spot for local artists and hipsters, as well as the budget-conscious families who opt to stay in the Fremont area. John's inability to relate to either crowd doesn't surprise me. So it's no shock he vetoed the place.

VETOED BY CURTAS

I'm not going to waste a lot of time on Firefly, because the management doesn't waste a lot of time trying to make the food any good. This place is popular with the under-40 crowd for one reason: It's cheap. You'll taste that cheapness in the stale bread, limp shrimp, and tepid meatballs that come to your table, and you'll gaze around the crowded place and wonder what in the world is bringing people here. They call

Vetoes

it a tapas bar, but the bartenders (and the management) have neither a sherry on the list nor a clue what fresh-made Spanish food is about. If you must, the food at the downtown location is marginally better than the one on Paradise Road. You've been warned.

MESA GRILL
Southwest

Caesars Palace
(702) 731-7731
mesagrill.com/lasvegas
Mon.-Fri., 11 a.m.-2:30 p.m.; Sat.-Sun., 10:30 a.m.-3 p.m.;
5-11 p.m., daily

NOMINATED BY MANCINI

Bobby Flay has single-handedly reinvented the way Americans look at chili peppers. His expertise in blending them with fruits, coffee, and various other ingredients to show off their subtleties, rather than just their heat, has made them more than just a source of redneck bragging rights about who can eat the most. I'll admit the chef can sometimes appear little more than a one-trick pony. But it's a damn good trick! Of course, if you've already burned off your taste buds with years of chili abuse, the subtle nuances of Mesa's food will probably be lost on you. Perhaps that's John's problem. But the rest of America owes it to themselves to see what it is that made Flay famous.

VETOED BY CURTAS

Nothing about this place is as good as its reputation. Regardless, Bobby Flay (or more accurately, Bobby Flay's celebrity) packs the joint noon and night with acolytes, wannabes, and rubes who can't resist the lure of a retread food that should be a lot better than it is. Everything on the menu sounds so promising—five-spice mole, red chile-curry sauce, ancho chile-honey glaze, etc.—that your mouth starts watering as your flaming expectations are raised. Then the food shows up and you notice the complex chile flavors are barely there (and dripped on with an eyedropper) and what's left is a piece of protein (of soul-crushing ordinariness) barely garnished with a green-chile this or a roasted-tomato

Eating Las Vegas

that. All of it barely reminding you why you bothered in the first place. Drown your sorrows with beer, wine, and tequila selections that are almost good enough to make you forget about the food. We used our veto power to keep Mesa Grill off the Essential 50 list, but Flay is too important a presence on the American food scene to be ignored, even if he runs restaurants as mediocre as this.

MIX   French

THEhotel at Mandalay Bay
(702) 632-7777
mandalaybay.com
6-10:30 p.m., daily

NOMINATED BY CURTAS

Alain Ducasse's Vegas outpost is one of the most dramatic restaurants in the world. From the décor to the grub that shows up on your plate, Mix is one of very few joints on the planet where the food matches the view. Is that food as finely tuned and hand-crafted as what's turned out by Guy Savoy and Robuchon? Of course not. But the cooking is solid, mildly creative, and well-suited to a high-volume place that screams dazzle factor, but doesn't want to provide too much of a challenge on the plate for the turistas. Finally, of course, there's that view. Yes, you're paying for dining in spectacular surroundings 64 floors up (costing $15 mil to build), but a more romantic venue you will not find. Gentlemen, if you can't score after a meal here, it's time to retire the hardware.

VETOED BY MANCINI

You know the old saying that you never get a second chance to make a first impression? Well, my first visit to Mix was so absolutely horrible that I just can't bring myself to return. I saw my waiter only when he took my order and returned at the end of the night with my check. Service was ridiculously slow. Nobody even noticed that four out of the five horribly fishy shrimp in my wife's absurdly expensive shrimp cocktail went completely uneaten. And when we were leaving, our server

Vetoes

117

never thought to return the coat my wife checked when we entered, so we were forced to hunt it down through the hostess. When I published my review, I received several emails from people who'd had similarly bad experiences. And a lot of people in the food industry quietly whisper that this place just tries to put out too many meals a night to deliver the kind of food and service people expect from an Alain Ducasse restaurant—or any place that charges these kinds of prices. If you're determined to take in Mix's breathtaking view and modern décor, save yourself some cash and frustration and stick with snacks in the lounge.

N9NE   Steak

Palms
(702) 933-9900
n9negroup.com
Sun.-Thurs., 5:30-10 p.m.; Fri.-Sat., 5:30-11 p.m.

NOMINATED BY JACOBSON

I can't believe this place has been left out of the Essential 50, because Barry Dakake is such a terrific steakhouse chef and so many celebrities show up in this dining room on a nightly basis. The owners of the Palms Casino, the Maloof family, also own the Sacramento Kings NBA franchise, so you'll see athletes from all the major sports dining here. And the food is terrific, even the so-called wet-aged steaks, which the chef prepares at ultra-high heat on a vertical broiler. Dakake is one of the most innovative steakhouse chefs I know. His popcorn shrimp in a Chinese takeout box, served with sauces on the side and chopsticks, is the best version of the dish I've ever tasted. How about Philadelphia cheesesteak-stuffed egg rolls or one of the best raw-seafood platters in town? Add to that the smoking hot hostesses, an excellent wine list, and great desserts, and it all adds up to a seminal Vegas steakhouse.

VETOED BY MANCINI

As someone who isn't a huge red-meat eater, I already fear there may be too many steakhouses in this book. But at least they each have something different that sets them apart from the others. N9NE is unique in one major way, but it isn't the kind of thing that turns me on. This is the most popular restaurant in town for celebrities who want to make sure they get a mention in the gossip columns and wannabe star-fuckers who are more interested in a Paris Hilton sighting than their meal. Perhaps that's why the place can get away with not offering a single cut of dry-aged beef, an unforgivable sin in my book for any place that wants to be viewed as a world-class steakhouse. If you love Hollywood hotties and don't care about the aging process of a slab of beef, I highly encourage you to check this place out. On the other hand, if you think an "essential" steakhouse should be more concerned with its meat than being a celebrity meat market, I'd pass.

ORIGIN INDIA   Indian

4480 Paradise Road
(702) 734-6342
originindiarestaurant.com
11:30 a.m.-11:30 p.m., daily

NOMINATED BY CURTAS

This is not your father's Indian restaurant. Nothing here tastes like it does in other run-of-the-mill Indian restaurants in town. Chef Kuldeep Singh's inventive and intriguing take on the cuisine of the sub-continent makes it the one Indian restaurant that rises above all others. He can salve your spirits and singe your sinuses splendidly with tandoori black tiger shrimp infused in ajwain seed and kaffir lime, or tender rare tandoori lamb chops, or corn-fed chicken-thigh tikka with coriander and basil sauce. From those descriptions, you can tell this is a spice-fest of the first order. Singh knows how to moderate the heat and seasonings to fit the dish. He can blow your head off with a vindaloo or a Goan gashi, but he enjoys mixing up his spice repertoire like a great baseball pitcher enjoys changing speeds. His house-made chutneys are a marvel, as are the spicy cocktails that come from the bar. Singh's Punjabi gram flour and vegetable dumpling in silky yogurt sauce finished with whole coriander seeds, chilies, cumin, and asafetida is so good it could make a vegetarian out of us, as could his eggplant crushed with cumin and ginger.

Vetoes

119

I hear Kuldeep Singh is quite creative, and I admit that the atmosphere is sublimated, a rare quality in an Indian restaurant. But I can't forget the demerits they received from the Health Department and I've been in too many dirty restaurant kitchens not to know how horrifying they can be. What's more, one of the owners called my wife, who speaks Hindi, on her cell phone continually, badgering her to bring me to the restaurant. When I finally complied, he refused to give me a check, then complained when I didn't pony up a review quickly. (I eventually wrote two.) If you want a great Indian meal, go to London.

PAYMON'S MEDITERRANEAN CAFE   Mediterranean

4147 S. Maryland Parkway
8380 W. Sahara Avenue
(702) 731-6030; (702) 804-0293
paymons.com
11-1 a.m., daily

NOMINATED BY MANCINI

The original Paymon's location, next door to UNLV, is an integral part of the local restaurant scene and failing to include it in this book would be a disgrace. Fair prices, above-average (although admittedly not perfect) Mediterranean cuisine, and what was probably the town's first hookah lounge, have made it a favorite of students and plenty of other locals for years. And before Steve Wynn's recent conversion to veganism (now reflected in his restaurants' menus), this was one of the few places in town to find good vegetarian food. I rarely put a lot of stock in newspaper reader polls. But the fact that Paymon's has been winning in multiple categories in just about every poll out there for well over a decade indicates just how beloved the place is of the local community. John's veto didn't surprise me. Hearing him try to explain why students like a restaurant, however, is hilarious—coming from a guy in an age bracket where he can't hear the word "hip" without thinking "replacement."

VETOED BY CURTAS

Mediocre-to-bad Mediterranean food, like mundane Mexican and insipid Italian, survives, even flourishes, in America for one primary reason: It's cheap. The second reason gringos flock to all three is because the fundamental ingredients and seasonings are strongly flavored (and appealing) enough to mask the mendacity. Subtlety, refinement, and good groceries usually get left in the old country, while the owners laugh all the way to the bank—caring not a whit that none of their fellow countrymen would be caught dead in their joints. Exhibit 1: Paymon's. Those having no baseline for comparison of what "Mediterranean" cuisines should bring to the table, i.e., students or cheapskates (Paymon's primary clientele), like, even love, Paymon's. They think hummus is supposed to taste like wallpaper paste and tabouli should be stale and always light on the lemons. Under-seasoned, overcooked, cheap kebabs? That's probably the way they make 'em in Morocco, or Syria, or wherever, right? What about those signature "Athens" fries— fresh one time and a soggy mess another? Owner Paymon Raouf can take solace (and make bank) in knowing his customers assume that's the way Greeks have been eating them since the city-states. Al's insistence on including Paymon's in the book is akin to a (formerly respected) film critic arguing *Caddyshack II* should be listed as an all-time great. If you want decent Mediterranean food, go to Crazy Pita, Khoury's, Yassou, or Hedary's.

Chocolate Truffles from Jean-Philippe Pâtisserie, Aria

Additional Recommendations

The following lists are our further suggestions for Las Vegas' top restaurants in the dozen categories that readers, neighbors, colleagues, family, friends, and total strangers ask us to recommend most often.

It wasn't necessary for us to agree on them; we each submitted our favorites in each category. Still, a number of the Essential 50 appear (and are cross-referenced by this book's page numbers) in the lists for further highlighting and indexing purposes. For example, it wouldn't make sense to create a list of Las Vegas' best pizzas without the inclusion of Settebello, even though it's also one of our 50 Best. The same with Burger Bar at Mandalay Bay in the burger category. Also, it's a handy reference to something specific in the Essential 50, such as the cocktail programs at American Fish, Sage, Sensi, and Yellowtail and the desserts at Robuchon's two restaurants, along with Le Cirque, Payard, Sage, and Simon. If a restaurant has more than one location, we've listed either its most prominent or the one closest to the Strip.

Note that Huntington Press (the publisher of this book) also maintains the LasVegasAdvisor.com website, which covers the Las Vegas dining scene extensively. There you will find lengthy and up-to-date listings of cheap eats, late-nite dining, and food and meal options in many more categories than appear here.

Cheap Eats

Aloha Specialties (California Hotel)
12 E. Ogden Avenue
(702) 382-0338

The Beat Coffeehouse
520 Fremont Street, Ste. 101
(702) 686-3164

Capriotti's Sandwich Shop (10 locations)
322 W. Sahara Avenue
(702) 474-0229

Chicago Hot Dogs on Rancho
1078 N. Rancho Drive
(702) 647-3647

So where do you go when you've only got a few bucks in your pocket and you want something that's not just satisfying, it's actually memorable? Here are the best places for a tasty but super-low-budget snack.

Artichoke Toasts at Firefly Tapas Kitchen & Bar

Firefly Tapas Kitchen & Bar (2 locations)
3900 Paradise Road
(702) 369-3971

Mix Zone Café
2202 W. Charleston Boulevard
(702) 388-0708

Old Vegas Spots

Battista's Hole in the Wall
4041 Audrie Street
(702) 732-1424

Bootlegger Bistro
7700 S. Las Vegas Boulevard
(702) 736-4939

Chicago Joe's
820 S. 4th Street
(702) 382-5637

**THE Steak House
at Circus Circus:**
see page 96

Coachman's Inn
3240 S. Eastern Avenue
(702) 731-4202

El Sombrero
807 S. Main Street
(702) 382-9234

THE Steak House at Circus Circus

Additional Recommendations

Golden Steer Steakhouse

Golden Steer
308 W. Sahara Avenue
(702) 384-4470

Hitching Post Steakhouse
3650 N. Las Vegas Boulevard
(702) 644-1220

Hugo's Cellar (Four Queens)
202 Fremont Street
(702) 385-4011

Italian-American Club Restaurant
2333 E. Sahara Avenue
(702) 457-3866

Michael's Gourmet Room (South Point)
9777 S. Las Vegas Boulevard
(702) 796-7111

Pamplemousse Le Restaurant
400 E. Sahara Avenue
(702) 733-2066

Piero's Italian Cuisine
355 Convention Center Drive
(702) 369-2305

In a town that implodes its history long before it can actually be called history, it's surprising to find a handful of flashbacks to the "good old days." The food may not always be as good as what's served by the newcomers, but all of these places offer a glorious glimpse of Vegas days gone by.

Eating Las Vegas

Celebrity/People Watching

Vegas is where the stars come to play and the rest of America comes to do things that would totally embarrass them if anyone at home ever found out. Here are some of the best places to take in the show.

Café Martorano (Rio)
3700 W. Flamingo Road
(702) 221-8279

CUT at Palazzo: *see page 14*

Enoteca San Marco (Venetian)
3355 S. Las Vegas Boulevard
(702) 677-3390

Fix (Bellagio)
3600 S. Las Vegas Boulevard
(702) 693-7223

Lavo (Palazzo)
3327 S. Las Vegas Boulevard
(702) 791-1800

Mon Ami Gabi (Paris)
3655 S. Las Vegas Boulevard
(702) 944-4224

N9NE Steakhouse (Palms)
4321 W. Flamingo Road
(702) 933-9900

Rao's at Caesars Palace:
see page 78

Simon at Palms Place:
see page 90

Kerry Simon with Slash, Palms Place

Sinatra (Encore)
3131 S. Las Vegas Boulevard
(702) 770-3463

Smith & Wollensky Steakhouse
3767 S. Las Vegas Boulevard
(702) 862-4100

Spago at Caesars Palace:
see page 94

Stack Restaurant & Bar (Mirage)
3400 S. Las Vegas Boulevard
(866) 339-4566

TAO Restaurant (Venetian)
3377 S. Las Vegas Boulevard
(702) 388-8338

Rihanna with Chef Barry Dakake at N9NE

Late Night

Las Vegas never sleeps. But far too many restaurants don't stay open late enough to serve you after a good show or a late night of clubbing. Here are a few that do, along with their closing hours.

FIRST Food & Bar (Palazzo)
3327 S. Las Vegas Boulevard
(702) 607-3478
1 a.m. weekdays, 4 a.m. weekends

Herbs & Rye
3713 W. Sahara Avenue
(702) 982-8036
3 a.m.

Eating Las Vegas

Munchbar (Caesars Palace)

3570 S. Las Vegas Boulevard
(702) 731-7731
Tues., Fri., and Sat. 4 a.m.,
other days 2 a.m.

Raku: *see page 76*

3 a.m.

Sake House Ichiza

4355 Spring Mountain Road, Ste. 205
(702) 367-3151
Mon.-Sat., 4 a.m.; Sun., 3 a.m.

Stratta (Wynn)

3131 S. Las Vegas Boulevard
(702) 770-3463
6 a.m.

Stratta's Wood-Fired Margherita Pizza

S'mores, FIRST Food & Bar, Palazzo

Tacos Mexico (2 locations)
1800 S. Las Vegas Boulevard
(702) 444-2288
24 hours

Wolfgang Puck Bar & Grill (MGM Grand)
3799 S. Las Vegas Boulevard
(702) 891-3000
6 a.m.

Burgers

Bachi Burger
470 E. Windmill Lane, Ste. 100
(702) 242-2244

BLT Burger (Mirage)
3400 S. Las Vegas Boulevard
(702) 792-7888

Bradley Odgen (Caesars Palace)
3570 S. Las Vegas Boulevard
(702) 731-7413

Burger Bar at Mandalay Bay; see page 42

KGB's custom burger, Harrah's

Sometimes all you want is a good old comforting hamburger. Fortunately, this town offers everything from fast-food fabulousness to gourmet beef on a bun. You'll find the best of the best at these places.

In-N-Out Burger
(multiple locations)
4705 S. Maryland Parkway
(800) 786-1000

KGB Kerry's Gourmet Burgers (Harrah's)
3475 S. Las Vegas Boulevard
(702) 369-5000

Mesa Grill
(Caesars Palace)
3570 S. Las Vegas Boulevard
(702) 650-5965

Stripburger's Blue Cheese Burger with Fried Onions

Smashburger (3 locations)
9101 W. Sahara Avenue
(702) 462-5500

Slidin' Thru
slidinthru.com

Stripburger
3200 S. Las Vegas Boulevard
(702) 737-8747

Pizza

Anthony & Mario's Broadway Pizzeria
840 S. Rancho Drive
(702) 259-9002

Ciao Ciao
4460 S. Durango, Ste. H
(702) 889-2700

Additional Recommendations

Grimaldi's (2 locations)
9595 S. Eastern Avenue, Ste. 100
(702) 657-9400

Metro Pizza (multiple locations)
4001 S. Decatur Boulevard
(702) 362-7896

Rao's at Caesars Palace:
see page 78

Settebello: *see page 88*

Las Vegans come from all across America, so our pizza represents every style the country has to offer. But for a true slice of heaven, check these out.

New Haven Clam Pizza, Ciao Ciào

Desserts

Aureole at Mandalay Bay: *see page 32*

FIRST Food & Bar (Palazzo)
3327 S. Las Vegas Boulevard
(702) 607-3478

Freed's Bakery (2 locations)
4780 S. Eastern Avenue
(702) 456-7762

Jean-Philippe Pâtisserie (Aria and Bellagio)
3600 S. Las Vegas Boulevard
(702) 693-8788

Joël Robuchon at MGM Grand: *see page 16*

L'Atelier de Joël Robuchon at MGM Grand: *see page 18*

Le Cirque at Bellagio: *see page 52*

Michael Mina (Bellagio)
3600 S. Las Vegas Boulevard
(702) 693-7223

Assorted pastries at Jean-Philippe Pâtisserie

Payard Pâtisserie Bistro at Caesars Palace: *see page 70*

Restaurant Guy Savoy at Caesars Palace: *see page 22*

Sage at Aria: *see page 82*

Simon at Palms Place: *see page 90*

Sometimes dinner is just a prelude to what a great pastry chef is whipping up in the kitchen. These are the places where you'll find the best desserts in the desert.

Additional Recommendations

Spring Mountain Road/Chinatown

Bosa 1 (Vietnamese)
3400 S. Jones, Ste. 2A
(702) 418-1931

Capital Seafood (Cantonese)
4215 W. Spring Mountain Road, Ste. B-202
(702) 227-3588

Crown Bakery
4355 W. Spring Mountain Road, Ste. 207
(702) 873-9805

Dong Ting Spring (Hunan)
3950 Schiff Drive
(702) 387-7888

Greenland Supermarket Food Court (Korean)
6850 W. Spring Mountain Road
(702) 459-7878

Honey Pig (Korean)
4725 W. Spring Mountain Road
(702) 876-0711

J & J Szechwan
5700 W. Spring Mountain Road, Ste. A
(702) 876-5983

Korean Garden BBQ
4355 W. Spring Mountain Road, Ste. 201
(702) 383-3392

Monta: *see page 62*

Head west from the Strip on the street between Treasure Island and the Fashion Show Mall to reach a neighborhood the locals call Chinatown. But that name is deceiving, because the area features incredible cuisine from all across Asia. A full tour could take years, but here are some good places to start.

Miso ramen at Monta

Mother's Korean Grill
4215 W. Spring Mountain Road, Ste. 107
(702) 579-4745

Noodle Café and Chinese Barbeque (Cantonese)
4355 W. Spring Mountain Road, Ste. 104
(702) 220-3399

Penang Malaysian
5115 W. Spring Mountain Road, Ste. 217
(702) 648-9889

Capital Seafood's
House Special lobster

Raku: *see page 76*

Sake House Ichiza (Japanese)
4355 W. Spring Mountain Road, Ste. 205
(702) 367-3151

Shuseki (Japanese)
5115 W. Spring Mountain Road, Ste. 117
(702) 222-2321

Yi Mei Champion Taiwan Deli
3435 S. Jones Boulevard
(702) 222-3435

Yunnan Garden (Szechuan/Yunnan)
3934 Schiff Drive
(702) 869-8885

Additional Recommendations

Sushi

BARMASA at Aria:
see page 10

Blue Fin Sushi & Roll
3980 E. Sunset Road
(702) 898-0090

Hachi (Red Rock Resort)
11011 W. Charleston Boulevard
(702) 797-7777

Japonais (Mirage)
3400 S. Las Vegas Boulevard
(702) 792-7979

Kai Sushi & Steak House
4246 S. Durango Drive
(702) 251-1520

Sushi can be deceptively simple. But the following places know what it takes to properly cut the highest-quality fish and team them with perfectly prepared rice.

Tuna Tartare at Shibuya, MGM Grand

Nobu (Hard Rock)
4455 Paradise Road
(702) 693-5090

Raku: *see page 76*

Sen of Japan: *see page 84*

Shibuya (MGM Grand)
3799 S. Las Vegas Boulevard
(702) 891-3001

Wazuzu (Encore)
3131 S. Las Vegas Boulevard
(888) 320-7110

Kani Nigiri at Japonais, Mirage

Yellowtail at Bellagio: *see page 108*

Beer

Crown & Anchor (2 locations)
4755 Spring Mountain Road
(702) 876-4733

Freakin' Frog
4700 S. Maryland Parkway
(702) 597-9702

Hofbräuhaus
4510 Paradise Road
(702) 853-2337

Rosemary's: *see page 80*

Two pints at Todd's English P.U.B.

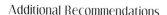
Additional Recommendations

Sage at Aria: *see page 82*

Tenaya Creek Brewery
3101 N. Tenaya Way
(702) 362-7335

Todd English P.U.B.
(Crystals, CityCenter)
3720 S. Las Vegas Boulevard
(702) 489-8080

Benjamin Franklin said, "Beer is proof that God loves us and wants us to be happy." If you agree, here are the best places in town to worship—assuming you want a multi-denominational service.

250 beers on tap at Yard House

Wine Bars

Double Helix (Palazzo)
3327 S. Las Vegas Boulevard
(702) 979-2325

Enoteca San Marco (Venetian)
3355 S. Las Vegas Boulevard
(702) 677-3390

Mon Ami Gabi, Paris

Hostile Grape (M Resort)
12300 S. Las Vegas Boulevard
(702) 797-1000

Julian Serrano at Aria: *see page 50*

Marché Bacchus: *see page 60*

Mon Ami Gabi (Paris)
3655 S. Las Vegas Boulevard
(702) 944-4224

Nora's Wine Bar & Osteria
1031 S. Rampart Boulevard
(702) 940-6672

Valentino (Venetian)
3355 S. Las Vegas Boulevard
(702) 414-3000

Finding a good wine list in a Las Vegas restaurant is about as tough as finding a slot machine in a casino. But on those evenings (or afternoons) when the grape is your first priority, your first stop should be one of these.

Hostile Grape, M Resort

Additional Recommendations

139

Cocktail Programs

American Fish at Aria:
see page 30

Downtown Cocktail Room
111 N. Las Vegas Boulevard
(702) 880-3696

Herbs & Rye
3713 W. Sahara Avenue
(702) 982-8036

Nora's Italian Cuisine
6020 W. Flamingo Road, Ste. 10
(702) 873-8990

Sage at Aria:
see page 82

Sensi at Bellagio:
see page 86

Yellowtail at Bellagio:
see page 108

"Brewer's Deportation"
at the Downtown Cocktail Room

Forget the martinis, the cosmos, and those giant plastic tourist cups filled with frozen slush. Las Vegas is in the midst of a cocktail renaissance and these are the places at the forefront.

Eating Las Vegas

Restaurant Index

Restaurant Index

Neighborhood Restaurants

More Restaurants

Restaurant Index

About the Authors

JOHN A. CURTAS has been Las Vegas' reigning voice of food and restaurant commentary on KNPR, Nevada Public Radio, for the past 15 years. During that time, he has also been the first restaurant critic for *Las Vegas Life* magazine and the *Las Vegas Weekly* (for which he still writes), as well as a variety of local publications. Nationally, he has written for *Time Out Las Vegas*, *Fodor's Las Vegas*, *Best Places Las Vegas*, and for John Mariani's *The Virtual Gourmet* (www.johnmariani.com). He's currently the restaurant critic for KLAS TV (CBS)–Channel 8 and is the man behind the "Eating Las Vegas" food blog (www.eatinglv.com). He's a voting member for the James Beard Foundation restaurant/chef awards and San Pellegino World's 50 Best Restaurants, as well as a frequent guest on Food Network programs, including two stints as a judge on "Iron Chef America." When not eating in and writing about more restaurants than anyone in the history of Las Vegas, he can be found in the city's courts, practicing law as an always-hungry commercial, business, and real-estate litigator.

AL MANCINI discovered his passion for food while living in New York City, where he attended law school by day, tended bar and made pizza at the infamous punk club CBGB by night, and explored the Big Apple's dynamic dining scene during every spare moment in between. For the past eight years, he's served as the restaurant critic for *Las Vegas Citylife*. He's also written extensively about food and dining for numerous local lifestyle publications, such as *944*, *Where*, *What's On*, *Desert Companion*, and *Luxury Las Vegas*, and has served as a contributor to the international guidebook *Time Out Las Vegas*. Al also spent 15 years as a full-time entertainment reporter for ABC News Radio. In 2001 he became ABC's first Las Vegas-based correspondent, covering all things related to Sin City. He still works for the network on a part-time basis, freeing up more of his time for dining.

About the Authors

MAX JACOBSON has had a rousing career spanning almost 30 years in food journalism, but he'll be happy to fly under the radar if he loses some weight. His career took flight in 1984, when he signed on at the *Los Angeles Times* as a writer on Chinese and Japanese food, and expanded into food and wine writing shortly thereafter. He was fortunate to arrive in Vegas when the food scene really began to blossom and has been a food writer and editor there since 1999. He lives in Henderson with his wife, without cats, dogs, or birds.

PHOTOGRAPH BY DENISE TRUSCELLO

From left: Max Jacobson, John Curtas, and Al Mancini hammer out their final selections in the 5-star Alex at Wynn Las Vegas.

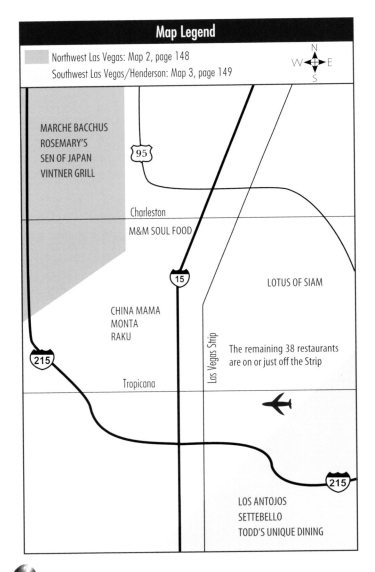

Map Legend

Northwest Las Vegas: Map 2, page 148

Southwest Las Vegas/Henderson: Map 3, page 149

MARCHE BACCHUS
ROSEMARY'S
SEN OF JAPAN
VINTNER GRILL

95

Charleston

M&M SOUL FOOD

15

LOTUS OF SIAM

CHINA MAMA
MONTA
RAKU

215

Las Vegas Strip

The remaining 38 restaurants
are on or just off the Strip

Tropicana

215

LOS ANTOJOS
SETTEBELLO
TODD'S UNIQUE DINING

Las Vegas Strip, Map 1

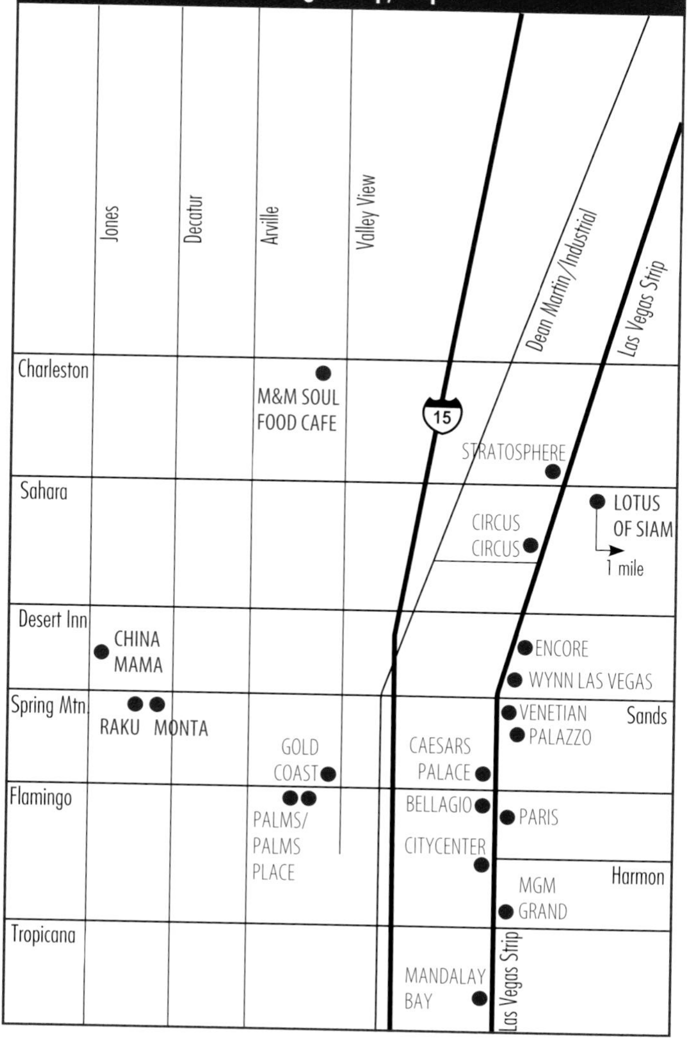

Jones

Decatur

Arville

Valley View

Dean Martin/Industrial

Las Vegas Strip

Charleston

● M&M SOUL FOOD CAFE

(15)

STRATOSPHERE ●

Sahara

● LOTUS OF SIAM

CIRCUS CIRCUS ●

→ 1 mile

Desert Inn

● CHINA MAMA

● ENCORE

● WYNN LAS VEGAS

Spring Mtn.

● ● RAKU   MONTA

● VENETIAN

● PALAZZO   Sands

GOLD COAST ●

CAESARS PALACE ●

Flamingo

● ● PALMS/ PALMS PLACE

BELLAGIO ●

● PARIS

CITYCENTER ●

MGM ● GRAND   Harmon

Tropicana

MANDALAY BAY ●

Las Vegas Strip

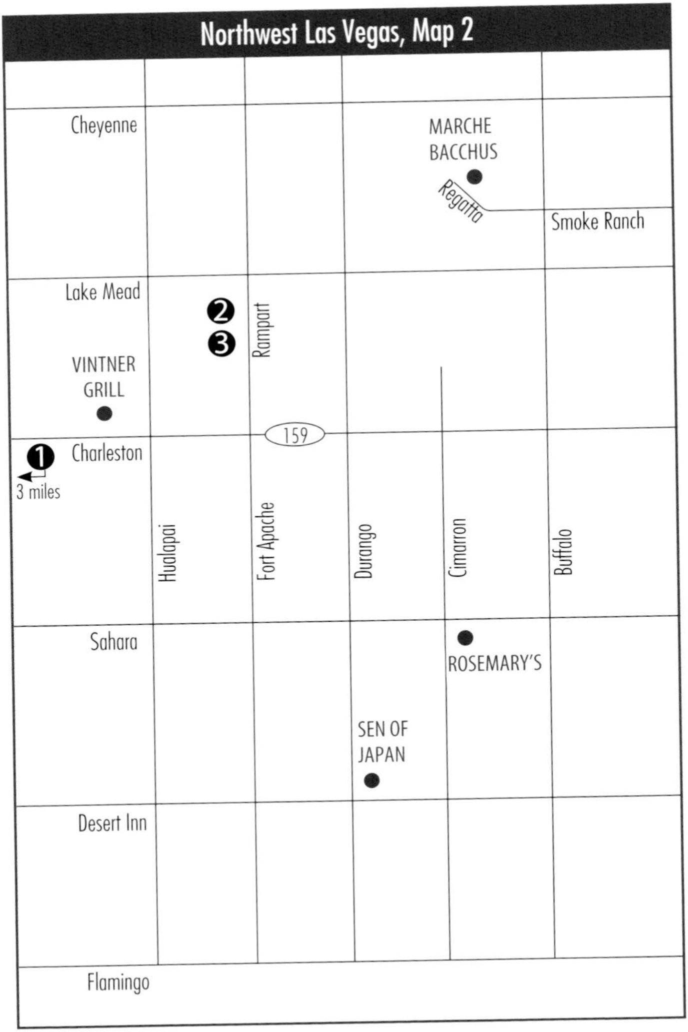

Northwest Las Vegas, Map 2

Cheyenne

MARCHE
BACCHUS

Regatta

Smoke Ranch

Lake Mead

2
3

Rampart

VINTNER
GRILL

1

3 miles

Charleston

159

Hualapai

Fort Apache

Durango

Cimarron

Buffalo

Sahara

ROSEMARY'S

SEN OF
JAPAN

Desert Inn

Flamingo

NEARBY CASINOS: RED ROCK RESORT (1), RAMPART (2), SUNCOAST (3)

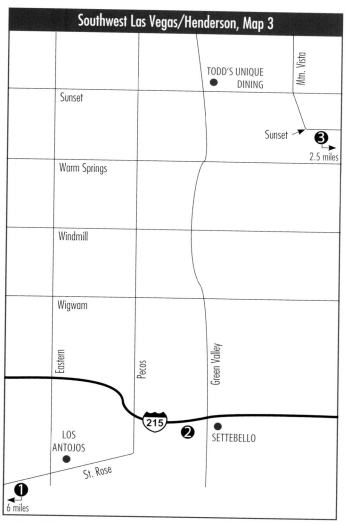

Southwest Las Vegas/Henderson, Map 3

TODD'S UNIQUE DINING

Mtn. Vista

Sunset

Sunset → ➌
2.5 miles

Warm Springs

Windmill

Wigwam

Eastern

Pecos

Green Valley

215

➋

LOS ANTOJOS

SETTEBELLO

St. Rose

➊
6 miles

NEARBY CASINOS: M RESORT (1), GREEN VALLEY RANCH (2), SUNSET STATION (3)

Eating Las Vegas

About Huntington Press

Huntington Press is a specialty publisher of Las Vegas- and gambling-related books and periodicals, including the award-winning consumer newsletter, *Anthony Curtis' Las Vegas Advisor*.

Huntington Press
3665 Procyon Street
Las Vegas, Nevada 89103
LasVegasAdvisor.com